Stories from the Bush

the Woodland Plays of De-ba-jeh-mu-jig Theatre Group

Compiled and Edited by
Joe Osawabine
with Shannon Hengen

Playwrights Canada Press
Toronto • Canada

Playwrights Canada Press
The Canadian Drama Publisher
215 Spadina Avenue, Suite 230, Toronto, Ontario M5T 2C7
416-703-0013   fax 416-408-3402
orders@playwrightscanada.com • www.playwrightscanada.com

The publisher acknowledges the support of the Canadian taxpayers through the Government of Canada Book Publishing Industry Development Program, the Canada Council for the Arts, the Ontario Arts Council, and the Ontario Media Development Corporation.

Production editor: Michael Petrasek
Cover designer: JLArt
Front cover photo courtesy of Ron Berti

Library and Archives Canada Cataloguing in Publication

Stories from the bush : the Woodland plays of De-ba-jeh-mu-jig Theatre Group / [compiled by] Joe Osawabine, Shannon Hengen.

Text mostly in English with some in Ojibway.
ISBN 978-0-88754-815-4 (bound)

1. Ojibwa Indians--Folklore--Drama. 2. Ojibwa Indians--Drama.
3. Canadian drama (English)--21st century. 4. Canadian drama (English)--Indian authors. I. Osawabine, Joe II. Hengen, Shannon Eileen III. De-ba-jeh-mu-jig Theatre Group.

PS8309.I53S76 2008   C812'.608037   C2008-901676-9

First edition September 2009
Printed and bound in Canada by Gauvin Press, Gatineau

"Brother Run," "Heritage," and
"Noweenagun" by Nadjiwan
reprinted with permission.

Table of Contents

Preface

As a theatre company, we have always known that we were doing something different up here on Manitoulin Island, than that which was happening in other regions of the country. We know we work differently. We know we operate from within a different set of values—an Aboriginal worldview holistic in nature, where all things are connected. Knowing there is a significant difference is one thing. Defining and articulating it, and turning it into a useful identification is another.

There are no other professional Aboriginal theatre companies in our region to look for a resemblance to. We spent many years trying to fit into mainstream models, measuring ourselves against our perception of other theatre companies in far-off urban lands, trying to validate the work we're doing as being on some level comparable, even though we knew deep inside that it was not. What we knew, was that there was another way of creating. We knew there were other stories than those being told in the mainstream. And we knew that in our collective past there was knowledge and experience and protocol and conventions and visioning and characters and all the essential elements that define theatre today, that have been in place for thousands of years.

We recently had opportunity to sit in conversations around the circle with Mr. Tom Peltier, in which he shared with us how in 1966 the Manitou Arts Foundation was formed by a small group of people, including himself, and the impact that had on the whole Woodland School, as it became known. The Manitou Arts Foundation was set up as a summer school held at Schreiber Island, with notable artists Daphne Odjig, Carl Ray, and Gerald Dokis providing mentorship for the young emerging artists who attended the school. Among the students at Schreiber Island were De-ba-jeh-mu-jig's co-founders Shirley Cheechoo and Blake Debassige. Both are still heavily involved in the arts and are still practising today and both have earned recognition as Aboriginal artists with unique visions and styles that indicate their origin in Manitoulin's Manitou Arts Foundation and the Woodland School of art.

De-ba-jeh-mu-jig certainly owes a great deal of gratitude to those artists who have paved the way for us to exist as we do today. Although the term "Woodland" has primarily been reserved for visual artists, and does suggest a very unique aesthetic, we found we easily self-identified with the term. While we may be practising in a different medium, we are, in fact, artists from the woodland, informed and inspired by the energy and beauty and spirit and knowledge of our natural woodland environment.

It was through the process of selecting the plays, introducing the works, and naming the collection that we came to the realization that this may actually be a distinct genre of Canadian plays. For over two decades we have heard the question (we have *asked* the question) "What is Native Theatre?" and no one has been able to answer. At least now, one thing we can say for sure is that the Woodland Plays are, at the very least, a significant part of the definition.

With the publication of the collection *Stories from the Bush: The Woodland Plays of De-ba-jeh-mu-jig Theatre Group,* our practice and our stories not only reach and influence many more people; we also further define our niche in a national context. To quote one of the works in the publication, "We are the images we create." Working in a cultural ecology that continues to validate and support the oral tradition, we sometimes need to be enticed or invited or escorted into participation in the text-based literary traditions, without which we remain invisible to the mainstream. We hope this collection will give readers a richer idea of what the world looks like from where we create—in the woodlands.

—Joe Osawabine

Woodland Theatre

by Shannon Hengen

Aabiish enjiibaayin? Nswakamok ndoonjibaa. What might it mean to pronounce those sentences—Where are you from? I am from Sudbury—in Ojibway in the heart of Ojibway country? It might mean that we are sensing, if only momentarily and vaguely, a deep connection with the people who have lived in this part of the continent from ancient times. And what might that connection mean? That we need to look no further than the culture of those people to understand fully what we're saying with the words, "I am from northern Ontario."

This collection of six Woodland plays by De-ba-jeh-mu-jig Theatre, a first, introduces us to Ojibway legends and what must have been a tradition of dramatizing them that date back millennia. Artistic Director Joe Osawabine and Artistic Producer Ron Berti have made the important connection between Woodland pictorial art and the plays that De-ba-jeh-mu-jig creates, bringing together in the term reference to all of the Aboriginal culture produced in the Great Lakes region over time. Norval Morriseau, in his book *Legends of My People, the Great Ojibway*, retells and illustrates many legends from the region, and it is with his name and art that the term "Woodlands" has become associated. He states in the book: "My people, be proud of your great societies, the Midaywewin and Wabinowin, and the great Ojibway Medicine Society of the Three Fires.... We... must write down and record legends, art, songs and beliefs not for ourselves alone but for all future Ojibway" (2, 3). *Stories from the Bush* does so.

De-ba-jeh-mu-jig Theatre has reached a quarter-century of theatre work on Manitoulin Island. Known for its highly innovative productions in the unique setting of the ruins of Holy Cross Mission in Wikwemikong Unceded Reserve, Debaj—as it is often called—brings together artists and practitioners from northern Ontario and well beyond in honouring its goal to enliven and preserve traditional Aboriginal culture. The plays collected here trace a continuity from the theatre's early years to the present: timeless legends of this place made vivid and real—often witty, always wise.

We must remember that these legends are rooted in the place where Debaj tells them. To experience them told here is to begin faintly to glimpse the region's earliest, still resonant teachings. In her study of the geography and culture in which Debaj works, Sophie Edwards writes:

> It is critically important to Aboriginal communities that the legends and stories be told at their related sites, not simply because of the rhetorical strength of the mnemonic, but because place is

> intrinsically linked with life, with history, with story, with the future. Walking upon a land narrated by story, one is reminded that we are part of a greater history, and that land continues to exist and witness, beyond and before our time, however mediated by our narrative. (126)

My study of the writing of contemporary anthropologist Julie Cruikshank confirms that, when facing large important issues, all human beings seem to look beyond themselves for guidance. Cruikshank lived in the Yukon and recorded the life stories of three female elders, publishing her first book under the title of *Life Lived Like a Story*. The women she interviewed and befriended taught her about how to construe their lives, and although the method of storytelling or personal disclosure derives from these Native women's specific language and culture, it bears a clear resemblance to the method of dramatic creation and production used at De-ba-jeh-mu-jig.

Cruikshank explains that "From the beginning, several of the eldest women responded to my questions about secular events by telling traditional stories. The more I persisted with my agenda, the more insistent each was about the direction our work should take. Each explained that these [legendary] narratives were important to record *as part of* her story" (2). "Each narrator," Cruikshank continues, "combines traditional narrative with individual experience to construct a coherent account of her life" (xi), and this combination becomes "the distinguishing feature of these life histories" (2). Just as the Yukon elders invoked traditional stories to explain turning points in their lives, the artists at Debaj weave legendary and personal accounts to create and produce their work. We who have access to the teachings presented by De-ba-jeh-mu-jig Theatre can similarly learn from them about our own lives.

In describing Cree performance culture with its ancient roots, Geraldine Manossa writes:

> Storytelling is about sharing the history and knowledge of the land, by recounting how beings since the beginning of time have interacted with it. …[W]e must know our own tribal songs and dances. It is up to us to conduct the necessary research. For the Native performer, the outcome… is the starting point for Native Performance Culture. We need to listen and learn from Great-granny stories. As artists we should be able to be inspired by our land's powerful beings, like Wasakaychak, Coyote, Raven, and Nanaboozoo. Salish writer/performer Lee Maracle reminds us that prior to the colonization of North America, there existed a theatre tradition for Native people. (178, 179)

Stephanie McKenzie in her book, *Before the Country: Native Renaissance, Canadian Mythology*, studies the relationship between Native and non-Native literature of the 1960s and 1970s in Canada, a time that she refers to as the

Native Renaissance. Though she cites few dramatic texts or performances, she nevertheless draws the significant conclusion about Native fiction and oratory of that period that it was in fact not "protest literature" as has been generally argued but rather wisdom literature. At a time—with the Canadian centenary and accompanying intensely nationalistic sentiment occurring—when mainstream artists and critics were beginning widely to acknowledge the absence of a Canadian mythology out of which to create great art, figures in the Native Renaissance were celebrating theirs.

With a humility appropriate to the general ignorance of mainstream culture about aboriginal art, McKenzie writes: "Many critics—mostly those non-Aboriginal—are not at the stage yet in the criticism of Aboriginal literatures to offer convincing theories about contemporary Aboriginal literatures or their anterior traditions" (178), and "Whatever words we choose to define the influence which Aboriginal writing has had on Canadian literature will probably be better chosen in the years to come" (186).

A collection such as *Stories from the Bush...* contributes to our education in "Aboriginal literatures" and is therefore invaluable. Consider the breadth of knowledge that we now have access to in these six tales. In *Lupi, The Great White Wolf*, as the Chief ages, he grows in wisdom and with good advice from his sister chooses to give his daughter in marriage not to the suitor with the biggest dowry but to the one with the truest heart. A vengeful grandmother intervenes, whose family had been killed by the Chief in war, demanding that the old engagement practice be honoured. But her grandson, the wolf, ends the violent retribution. "Watch the wolves," is the teaching that we hear in *The Indian Affairs*, a play in three acts. Two wolves in fact observe the humans throughout. Six characters meet at ages 8, 18, and 28, and in these three meetings at what was once their clubhouse on the reserve they feel a tension between their lives in the contemporary world, in the city or on the reserve, and the seven traditional values implied in the teaching: love, honour, respect, truth, trust, compassion, patience. They remain loyal to their childhood pledge to be friends forever.

New World Brave is a piece with an almost continual soundtrack, one whose refrain is "heal the circle that was broken and you'll find your wounds will mend." Five young men search for ways to bring ancient teachings into their complex contemporary lives, on the reserve and in the city. Images—some authentic, some misleading, all powerful—frame the piece. To quote from it: "we are the images we create." In *New Voices Woman* the protagonist is nameless until she overcomes fears and dangers, earns her medicine pouch, and finds her song. "New Voices Woman" both expresses self-knowledge and, because she is androgynous, points towards the renewal of tradition. Music has great power in this story, speaking to deep desires, as does love; both must be valued. The real and powerful perils of greed, on the other hand, must be overcome, and life protected. The spectacle of ugliness depicted and of figures changing forms provide vivid theatre.

The nine traditional stories in *Ever! That Nanabush!*, as told by Daphne Odjig, teach lessons about how best to survive and thrive. Beware, they say: much trickery occurs; and, know your limitations. Animals and plants are given their traits as protection (roses) or as reminders of betrayal (rabbits, raccoons). Mutual sustenance despite weather, lack of food or aging results from cooperation. In *The Gift*, a "one-act," a storyteller/actor relates the Frog Monster legend in which Manitoulin Island is created and the medicine pouch of a Nameless Man in the legend spilled over the island. On Manitoulin, where De-ba-jeh-mu-jig Theatre is located, many medicines still grow. The storyteller takes what he needs from the legend and in performing it invites the audience to do the same. What or who is the Frog Monster who prevents water from flowing? What is your name?

Works Consulted

Cruikshank, Julie. *Life Lived Like a Story: Life Stories of Three Yukon Native Elders.* Lincoln: University of Nebraska Press, 1990.

—. *When the World Began: A Yukon Teacher's Guide to Comparative Local Mythology.* Whitehorse: Government of Yukon Territory, Department of Education, 1978.

Edwards, Sophie. "La Cloche: Passage and Place." MA Thesis. Laurentian University, 2008.

Hengen, Shannon. *Where Stories Meet: An Oral History of De-ba-jeh-mu-jig Theatre.* Toronto: Playwrights Canada Press, 2007.

Johnston, Basil. *Ojibway Ceremonies.* Toronto: McClelland and Stewart, 1982, 1987.

—. *Ojibway Heritage: The Ceremonies, Rituals, Songs, Dances, Prayers and Legends of the Ojibway.* Toronto: McClelland and Stewart, 1976, 1998.

—. *Tales the Elders Told: Ojibway Legends.* Paintings and drawings by Shirley Cheechoo. Toronto: Royal Ontario Museum, 1981.

Manossa, Geraldine. "The Beginning of Cree Performance Culture." *(Ad)dressing our Words: Aboriginal Perspectives on Aboriginal Literatures.* Ed. Armand Garnet Ruffo. Penticton, BC: Theytus Books, 2001. 169-180.

McKenzie, Stephanie. *Before the Country: Native Renaissance, Canadian Mythology.* Toronto: University of Toronto Press, 2007.

Morriseau, Norval. *Legends of My People, The Great Ojibway* [illustrated and told by Norval Morriseau]. Ed. Selwyn Dewdney. Toronto: The Ryerson Press, 1965.

Lupi, The Great White Wolf

Lupi, The Great White Wolf was written by Larry E. Lewis with Esther Jacko, based on Ojibway legend as told by Annie Migwanabi. Translated by Justine Enosse and Violet Naokwegijig.

Lupi, The Great White Wolf was originally produced in 1991 by De-ba-jeh-mu-jig Theatre Group, with the following company:

Harvey Bell Jr.
Jonathon Debassige
Justine Enosse
Gloria Eshkibok
Gregory Fisher
Jonathon Fisher
Rona George
Shannon Manitowabi
Bruce Noakwegijig
Clayton Odjig
Joe Osawabine
Leroy Peltier
Crystal Lynn Shawanda
Ruby Trudeau

Director:	Larry E. Lewis
Stage Management:	Jeffery Trudeau
Lighting Design:	Hugh Conacher
Sound Design:	Marsha Coffey
Set and Costumes:	Linda Leon
	Bill Shawanda

Characters

Young Warriors:
EBIITONG—like a guard or caretaker
CHI-GIMAANS (chief's son)
ADDIK
NIMKII

Young Women:
BIIDAABAN
DAANIS
NANGOONS

GCHI-GIMAA (chief to the village)
NGASHI (sister to the chief, aunt of Nangoons, mother of Ebiitong)
MDIMOOYEH (grandmother to Lupi)
LUPI
MA'IINGAN (LUPI in human form)
ZHASHK (voice-over)

Outline of Writing System

Vowels:

3 Short Vowels		English sounds		4 Long Vowels		English sounds
Ojibwe		English sounds		Ojibwe		English sounds
i	nzid	pin		ii	giin	see
a	sab	canoe		aa	naanan	father
o	nimosh	spoken		oo	goon	soon
				e	kwe	jet

Consonants:

b	d	g	j	z	zh
p	t	k	ch	s	sh
m	n	w	y		

Other sounds:
Nasal "**n**" (through nose)
    written as "**nh**" at ending of a word, e.g., "binoojiinh"
    written as "**n**" inside of a word, e.g., "binoojiins," "jaanzh"
Glottal Stop   **'** or **h**
    catch in the throat (ode')
"**ay**" (as in "mood**ay**" or "jiib**ay**")

Lupi, The Great White Wolf

ACT I

NANGOONS   Miigwech. [*Thank you.*]

NGASHI   Ngii-nsidaayendaami gii-ngashyaang maanda gwa naa kwezenswiyan. Kweng kii-bi-zhi-bskaabii. Aapji nminwaangwendaami. Giin nji bemaadzijig da-ni-bmaadziwag. [*You left as a girl; you return as a woman. We sorrowed when you departed, leaving behind a girlhood we had grown to love. We rejoice at your return, new and different. Through you, will the people live and live on.*]

   Scene shifts.

ADDIK   Washmen ii gwa ndinendam ji-ndownag Nangoons. [*I'd rather be catching Nohngose in my net.*]

EBIITONG   Aangwaamzin. Nimkii biidaasmose. [*Be careful. Here comes Nimke.*]

ADDIK   Oo; Nangoons, aaniipiish yaayan? Aapji gzaagin Nangoons. [*Oh Nohngose, where are you? I love you, Nohngose.*]

NIMKII   Kiibaadis. Gaayii kii-gkendziin zaagidwin. [*You fool. You don't know anything about love.*]

EBIITONG   Nigaazi Nimkii. Enso-noondang wi noozwin mii gwa eta... (*sighs*)... [*Poor Nimke. When he hears her name he sighs, and sighs, and sighs.*]

NIMKII   Zaagidwin nwiijkiwendig aapji gwa niizaanad. Kimoodmigwan naanaagdawendmowin midkizomagad oodi nsow gaad. [*And he calls me a fool! Love, my friends, is a very dangerous thing. It steals your brains right out of your head and hides them between your legs.*]

CHI-GIMAANS   Naanaagdawendmowin temgadni nsowgaad. [*His brains are between his legs.*]

NIMKII   Giin sa gwa naa gda-pabnan. [*And you are sitting on your brains.*]

CHI-GIMAANS   Mii na giiyenh. Begish bwaa-baagshkamaa. [*Is that so? I hope I don't squash them.*]

EBIITONG   Gda-poogzamig sha maaba. Gaayii kii-gkendziin. [*He is teasing you and you don't even know it.*]

CHI-GIMAANS   Gdoo-poogzam na? [*Are you teasing me?*]

NIMKII   Gnimaa gwa. Naaniibwin nwiijkiwenh. Ka-nwebtoon gnib-waakaawin. [*Maybe. You better stand up, friend, and give your brains a rest.*]

CHI-GIMAANS   Nangoons!

EBIITONG   Kinwaabmig wa kwezens. [*She's looking at you.*]

BIIDAABAN   Geget sa naa gewiinwaa gondag gwiizensag gwetaani gtimaadziwag. Giishpin giigoonh wii-mwongwaa giinwi gwa aabdig kwii-baa-nda-giigoonkemi. [*These boys are so lazy. If we want to eat fish, we have to catch them ourselves.*]

ADDIK   Begish zhi-gnawaabmid ezhi-gnawaabmaad Nimkii. [*I wish she would look at me the way she looks at Nimke.*]

NIMKII   Aanii giiyenh ekdoyan. Gaawii gnigenh wiikaa Nangoons nginwaabmigsii. Gaawiin ngii-gkenmigsii bmaadziyaang. [*What are you saying? Nohngose never looks at me. She doesn't even know I'm alive.*]

ADDIK   Pane kanwaabmig. Pii gwa wii-negwaabmad mii gegii nookkweseyan gzidenyan kanwaabdaman. Gnimaa nendmadig zaagtooyan gzidenyan. [*She's always looking at you. Until you look at her, then when she turns to look at you, you quickly stare at your toes. Probably she thinks you're just in love with your feet.*]

NIMKII   Ndaa-de-gaachida'mii na gwa? [*Do you think there's a chance for me?*]

EBIITONG   Ka-waamda'aa nongwa naagshig giishpin piichide'yan aanii enendman. [*Show her how you feel tonight if you're brave enough.*]

ADDIK   Giishpin bwaa-zhichigeyan niin nga-wiindmawaa. [*If you don't, I will.*]

CHI-GIMAANS   Aaniish iidig nbwaakaawin gaa-zhi-niisbideg ndiyaang! [*I wonder how my brains got into my bum!*]

EBIITONG   Ka-waabmigoo nongwa naagshig, Nimkii, miish ji-gkendman aanii ezhchigeng. [*We'll be watching you, Nimke, to learn how it's done.*]

CHI-GIMAANS   Ka-waabmigoo nongwa naagshig, Nimkii. Baabiiwshig! Aaniipiish ezhaayeg? [*See you tonight, Nimke. Hey, wait for me! Where are you going?*]

All exit except NIMKII, who speaks alone.

NIMKII   Noondmaa maanda nbiish mdawejiwang mii gwa ezhi-noon-doonaa baapyan Nangoons. Maaba ge giizis skaasang maanda nbiish dagowesing mii gwa ezhi-waabminaa gegii paa-naaniimyan. Aapji gwa mnooshkneshkaagwan maanda ezhi-zaaginaa Nangoons. [*When the waters slide over the rocks, I hear your laughter, Nohngose. You're in the air I breathe, smile through the night until the sun rises, warm and friendly to me. Dance, and the moonbeams touch the waving waters. My heart is full, Nohngose. So full of love for you that I feel sick.*]

Scene shifts.

GCHI-GIMAA   Ngii-moonenmaag gwa gonad niizh. Ngwekwendaan sha gwa nongwa iidig zaagidwaad. Manj dash ge-zhi-zhiikaazgwenh pii ndawendaagwak wi dbinweziwin. [*I was getting worried about those two, and my suspicions are correct. They are very much in love. The dowry settlement should prove very interesting.*]

NGASHI   Aanii dash maanda gdizhtwaaninaa waa-biidood washme dbinweziwin bkinaage. [*What are you saying? Tradition says the man with the largest dowry wins.*]

GCHI-GIMAA   Enh. [*Yes.*]

NGASHI   Gdikid na wii-miigweyan maaba gdaansenh zaagidwin nji? [*Are you saying that you will give your daughter's hand for love?*]

GCHI-GIMAA   Gaawii gwa myaa ndikdosii, eta gwa nda-zhi-waamdaan wi. [*I am not saying anything, just making an observation.*]

NGASHI   Gmino-gimaaw. Giin gwa eta gashtoon wii-bnaajtooyan maanda gdizhtwaaninaa. [*If anyone can break tradition, you can. You are a good chief.*]

GCHI-GIMAA   Ka-wiindmawnim nwiijkiwendig. Maaba ndaanis giizhiitaa wii-wiidigemaaganid. Nga-daapnamwaa dbinweziwin baajgaadegin jibwaa mooshkneyaasged miinwaa bezhig dbik-giizis. Mii maanda ezhi-wiindmoongok. [*My friends, my daughter is ready to become a wife. I will receive dowry proposals by the end of the next full moon. This message is to all who would join my family. I have spoken.*]

NGASHI   Ke-baabii'shin Nangoons. Gegoo ngii-mkwendaan waa-gwej-maag koos. [*I remember something I wanted to ask your father. Wait for me, Nohngose.*]

Scene shifts.

NANGOONS   Gaa gwa wiikaa nga-maamninaammigsii, ngii-nendam. [*I thought you would never notice me.*]

NIMKII   Edo-binoojiinwiying gmaamninaammin. [*I have noticed you since we were children.*]

NANGOONS   Aaniish miinwaa pii waa-waabminaa? [*When will I see you again?*]

NIMKII   Mii gwa baamaa pii giizhiitaamgak naaknigewin Nangoons. Aapji gwa baatiinad waa-nonkiiyaanh giishpin wii-bkinogwaa nwiijninwag. Gegwa zegzike. Ka-wiidgemin gwa. [*Not until the day of the proposals. I have a lot of work to do if I'm going to beat out the other men. I won't fail, Nohngose. You're going to be my wife.*]

NANGOONS   Gaa gwa wiya bekaanzid nga-baabiiyaasii Nimkii. [*I will wait for no other, Nimke.*]

NGASHI   Wegnesh naa gaa-biindgeshkaagyan? Aaniish gwa naa ezhiyaayan? [*What spirit has entered you?*]

NANGOONS   Nimkii ngii-waawiindmaag nongwa enaagshig wii-ni-aabji-zaagidyaang. [*The spirit of crazy love. Tonight Nimke pledged himself to me.*]

NGASHI   Nangoons! Gegwa sa mi-jaanmendange. Koos nii wi wii-dbaaknige'endaan waa-wiidgemad nini. [*Oh, little Nohngose, don't be hasty. Your father is the one who will decide who your husband will be.*]

NANGOONS   Gbooksenmin nashenh ji-ke-naadmawyan. Pane gwa gbizindaag noos. [*Speak to him, Auntie. Plant a seed in his heart. He always listens to you. Goodnight, my beautiful auntie.*]

NGASHI   Ezhi-gshkitoowaanh nga-zhichige giishpin nishing nendmaa. [*I'd plant a whole crop if I thought it would help.*]

> The women retreat and we focus on the CHIEF. His son enters.

GCHI-GIMAA   Giin waa nangoonsdig ngamyeg mii gwa waaseyaanziyeg. Mkade-bneshiinyag gdaawim. Naaw-giizhig pane gbimbizom. Waa'aaskoneyeg mii gwa dbishko debtaagziyeg. [*You are the stars that sing, you sing with your light. You are the birds of fire, you fly over the sky. Your light is the voice, you make a path to pass over.*]

CHI-GIMAANS   Noos! Noos! Wewiib maajaan! [*Father! Father! Come quickly!*]

GCHI-GIMAA   Nimkii-bnesi, gegoo na gwa kidwin gda'aan niin nji. Giigdan. Pane gwa oodi gidaapkaan paa-zhaa'aanh nwaamdaanan niwi gda-zaswinan, gaa'sh gwa wiikaa kii-waabmisnoo. [*If you have words for me, thunderbird, then speak. I have often seen your nests, hollowed in stones on the cliffs, but never have you shown yourself to me.*]

CHI-GIMAANS   Aaniish gaa-kidod? [*Did you hear what was said?*]

GCHI-GIMAA   Gaa gegoo gii-kidsii. [*No, I didn't catch it. I must learn to listen better.*]

CHI-GIMAANS   Aaniish maaba Nimkii-bnesi bebaa-ndoo-dwewed nongwa iidig gewii, gnimaa ge da-mbinaan zhinda gitkamig. Oo, da-nishin gdaapkaan ji-baa-zhaaying ji-oo-nbwaachi'ang Nangoons. [*Maybe the thunderbird came down from the mountains to check out Nohngose. Maybe he'll fly away with her to the land above the earth. Maybe I'll get to visit her there. That would be great.*]

GCHI-GIMAA   Aapji gwa ngwiininendam ngwisenh. Maanda aabig nii-naanaagdawendaan waa-naabying. Maanda wii-ni-bmaadziying nji. [*I'm worried, son. I must keep my vision clear now. Our lives will depend on it.*]

> MDIMOOYENH enters. Scene shifts.

MDIMOOYENH   Daapnan maanda gaa-biidoowaanh naaknigewin. [*Accept this proposal.*]

GCHI-GIMAA   Wenesh maaba bebaa-waawiindmaaged wii-niibwitwaad ndaanis Nangoons? [*Who offers such a dowry for my only daughter, Nohngose?*]

MDIMOOYENH   Niin nda-aankanootmawaa nooshenh wii-wiidgoowaad niwi gdaanis. [*I do, on behalf of my grandson, so that he may have your daughter's hand in marriage.*]

GCHI-GIMAA   Maanoo win da-giigdodmaadzo gooshenh. [*Let your grandson speak for himself.*]

MDIMOOYENH   Gaawiin maaba giigdosii. Niin nda-aankanootmawaa. [*He cannot speak. He has been that way since early childhood. I speak for him.*]

NANGOONS   Wenseh gonad bemaadzijig? [*Who are these people?*]

NGASHI   Gaa ngii-gkenmaasiig. Myekkwonyewag. Jibwemwag saw ii gwa. [*I don't know. Their dress and accent are unusual, yet they speak Ojibway.*]

NANGOONS   Gwaabmaa na wa shkiniigish? Zegnaagdinwan niwi shkiinzhigoon. [*Look how wild his eyes are.*]

GCHI-GIMAA   Gdoo-kwejim dash ndaan wii-niibwitwaad nini gaagdosig. [*You ask me to marry my daughter to a man who cannot speak?*]

MDIMOOYENH   Gii-gchi-nokii maaba mnik kina gegoo eyang. Niibnanching zhinda gii-zhiibaashkaa mnising paa-aashtoonged mii gii-waabmaad niwi gdaanis. Nongwa dash nandwenmaan wii-wiidgoowaad. Gaa na gwaadazin mnik ge-ndinmawaad; gegii gwa ka-bsenmaa? [*Look! He has worked hard to gather this dowry. Many times he has passed your way during trade and noticed your fair daughter. He desires her for his wife. Can you not see he will provide well for her and make you a rich man also?*]

Yaa na gwa geyaabi shkiniigish ge-bkinwaad ninda nooshenyan? Giishpin eyaagwenh da-giigdo? [*Is there a man here who can match the dowry offered by my grandson? If there is, let him speak.*]

NIMKII   Gimaa, maanda genii ngii-biidoon naaknigewin. [*Chief, I present my proposal.*]

Miinwaa dash bekish nwaawiindmaagen zaagidwin miinwaa maanda bmaadziwin. [*In addition to what you see before you, I offer Nohngose my love and my life.*]

GCHI-GIMAA   Aabdig gwa maanda nii-naanaagdawendaan naaknigewin. Gbagdinin'sh maampii wii-baabiiyan endnakiiyaang. [*I will consider your offer with the rest. You are welcome to wait in our village.*]

MDIMOOYENH Gminaadenmimi gwa. Zhaazhi ngii-zhisdoonaa waa-dnizyaang mnishensing epangishmog nikeying. [*You honour us. But we have made our camp on the neighbouring island to the west.*]

GCHI-GIMAA Gnabaj gwa gbeying maanda da-njitaamgad, baatiindoon gwa ninda waa-dbaamdamaanin jibwaa naaknige'endmaa waa-zhiwe- bak. [*It may take me longer than expected to make a decision. There are so many offers.*]

MDIMOOYENH Aahaaw. Gaa sha wii gwa zaam gbeying. Waasa gwa nii-zhaami wii-ni-giiweyaang. [*Very well. But do not keep us waiting long. We have a great distance to travel after this.*]

NANGOONS Aaniish waa-zhichigeying? [*What are we to do?*]

NIMKII Kina go gegoo eyaamaa miinwaa niin ngii-toon. Giishpin debsesnog ndawaaj gwa naa ka-gjiboowemi. [*I have presented all that I have and am. If it is not enough, then will you come with me and defy your father?*]

NANGOONS Aahaaw. Aaniipii dash ge-zhaaying? [*Yes. But where would we go?*]

NIMKII Oo, ngoji sa gwa naa ge-nji-mkaagooswang. [*To a place where we cannot be found.*]

NGASHI Nangoons! Gegwa giibaajchigeke. [*Nohngose, don't be foolish now!*]

NANGOONS Noos, Nimkii nzaagaa. Gegwa dash miigweke niiyaw. Ngwasaa nii go wa nini. Gaa go maamdaa ji-bmaadziyaambaa giishpin bwaa-wiigendwag Nimkii. [*Please do not give me to this strange man as a wife. He frightens me so. It is Nimke I love, dear father. I shall die without him.*]

NANGOONS exits.

GCHI-GIMAA Mii gwa dbishko gaa-dshinin waa'aashkeshiins ezhi-gnawaabmigoowaanh. [*The eyes of a wounded doe look up at me.*]

NGASHI Aaniish gwa naa. [*Well.*]

GCHI-GIMAA Ndawemaa, aaniish iidig ge-zhichigeyaanh? Gaawii go washme gii-biidoosiin niwi wi'sh mnik mdimooyenh gaa-biidood. [*Sister, what am I to do? No one has brought me a larger dowry than the old woman.*]

NGASHI Geget sa aanwi. Gaa wiya washme gii-biidoosiin. Nda-zhi- waamdaan sa wii gwa maanda zhinda wiya bekaanzid gii-biidood nwanj wenjishing. [*No one brought a larger dowry, but I noticed someone who brought one better in quality.*]

GCHI-GIMAA   Getin gii-nokii Nimkii. Miish go eta maaba mdimooyenh gbishin. Maanda ge zhitwaawin gaawii nii-bnaajtoosiin. [*Nimke has worked hard. If it wasn't for the old woman, I could have chosen him. I cannot break tradition.*]

NGASHI   Daa-aanjchigaade sa ge gwa naa maanda zhitwaawin, aanind gonda gwiiji-nishnaabemnaanig gaawii minwaangosiinaawaa. [*What a foolish tradition. It should be changed. Some traditions can make people so unhappy.*]

GCHI-GIMAA   Nga-giibaadenmigoog gonda bemaadzijig giishpin zhi-bgidnag Nimkii wii-niibwitwaad. [*I will lose the respect of my people if I let her marry Nimke.*]

NGASHI   Washme sa nii go naa gdaa-minaadenmigoo nsidwinman wi zaagidwin. Ka-waamdawaag gonda bemaadzijig aanii ezhi-ode'yan. [*You will gain further respect instead by recognizing the dowry of love as well. Show your people your heart and its humility.*]

GCHI-GIMAA   Nii-daapnamwaa maaba Nimkii naaknigewin. *(all kids say...*"NIMKII"*...)* Maaba ge ndaanis da-mno-zhiyaa. Maanda ge ngodooeziwin gaa wiikaa ka-'ni'aasiinaa. [*I will accept the offer of Nimke. In this way I will make my daughter happy and our tribe will not lose its fair flower.*]

       Scene shifts.

NIMKII   Nangoons, niin Nimkii. [*Nohngose, it is I, Nimke.*] *(some kids say...*"Shtaa-taa-haa!"*...)* Maanda nbiidoon wii-mkwendaman maanda kaagige zaagidwin, mii gwa dbishko waakaagan. [*These are for you. Let this strand remind you of our love and how eternal it shall be, like the circle.*]

NANGOONS   Geget gwenaajwang. Nwaamdaanan nanda danowa, nwiijkwewag nwaamdamwaag mshkimdensing wiinwaa da-toonaawaa. Epiichi-gchiendmaa. Mii gwa ji-biiskamaa. [*No other woman in the tribe has such a valuable article. I have seen the beginnings of a strand some women keep in pouches. I am so proud.*]

NIMKII   Ntam ge-ndaadzid bezhig nga-aankesdowaa. [*I will place a new strand next to this when our first child is born.*]

EBIITONG   Aahaaw! Maajtaadaa wii-niibwichigeying. [*Let the wedding begin!*]

NIMKII   Aambe Nangoons. Oo-niibwidaa. Ka-mnaajtoonaa maanda wii-gchitwaa-giizhgakeying. [*Come, Nohngose. They are waiting for us. Let's marry and feast and enjoy this great day.*]

ADDIK   Mii go maanda debwewin. Gimaa gii-miigwenan daansan Nangoons wii-niibwitwaad Nimkiin. [*It is the truth. Our chief has given his daughter Nohngose in marriage to Nimke.*]

MDIMOOYENH   Wiindmaw wa Gchi-gimaa. Gaa go gnigenh maanda nmino-daapnasiin kidwin. Wiindmaw Gchi-gimaa ji-aandaaknige'endang. Nga-zhichige ji-gchi-giisaadendang. Ni-maajaan! [*Tell your great chief: I do not accept this news. Tell your great chief to change his decision. Or I will make him live to regret it. Go!*]

Mnidoog, bzindaw maaba mdimooyenh. Ezhi-niizhyaang ngii-shkwamnigoomnaaba. Maaba gii-binoojiinwid ngii-bi-gbannigoomnaaba oodi waabnang egwindeg mnis yaad nini. Gii-biinaabiniin danniiman; kina go gegoo gii-bnaajtoonaawaaba. Ezhi-gshkitoowaanh, ngii-bgosenmaa wii-shkonnaad nanda binoojiinyan. Miish go wi pii gaa-ko-giigdosiig. Ngii-zhi-ndawaabndaan gaa-zhi-nigaagoowaang wii-daapnin niwi daansan. Mii gii-oo-niigwed bekaanzinjin. Gaa'sh gnigenh da-zhiwebsinoo enendang. Nooshenh, giin go ka-djbenmaa wa Nangoons. Daapnan wi ma'iingni-ndib, wiikwejiipzon niwi ma'iingniyaanan, jiigi-shkodeng kazhingishin. Ndaa'aan go wi mshkiki ji-naachigeyaanh maanda gaa-zhinigaagooyan. Aashtowaawewin! [*Gods, listen to this old woman. We are all that is left of our tribe. When this child was a baby, an attack was led against us by that chief over there on the next island. He and his men destroyed everything. It was I who begged him to spare the life of this child. This child has never spoken since that night. I sought to amend my grief over this by taking his daughter. Now he has given her to another. But, he will not have his way. Grandson,*]

Painting by Blake Debassige.

Nohngose will be yours. Hold to your heart the wolf's head. Wrap yourself in skins and lay by the fire. I have medicine to change these wrongs that have been done to you. Revenge!]

ACT II

NIMKII   Aaniish ezhwebak? [*What is the matter?*]

NANGOONS   Nbizinzhe. [*I am listening to the night.*]

NIMKII   Ma'iingan go naa eta ewaa'oonaad dbik-giizoon. [*It is only a wolf howling at the moon.*]

NANGOONS   Gaawiin maaba ma'iingning zhiyaasii. Gaa ge nwesii. Dbikong aapji gii-nchiiwad. Gaa'sh go gnigenh gii-gmiwzinoo. Gegoo nda-zhi-manis. Bizinshen Nimkii. Wiijgendwishin. [*This was no ordinary wolf. It was as if he wanted to become the moon during the night of a fierce storm that gave no rain. This is a message to you. Listen, Nimke. Stay with me.*]

NIMKII   Gaawii maamdaa. Aabdig sa gwa nii-paa-aashtoonige, wii-yaamang waa-nakaazying waa-dnizying. Nbogsendam wii-mingiizhgak. Jibwaa zoogpok ka-wiijgendaadmi. [*I have to trade so you have what you need for our lodge. And I need the good weather. We will be together long before winter.*]

NANGOONS   Pane sa ge gwa. [*And always.*]

NIMKII   Aaniipiish ezhaayan? [*And where are you going?*]

    As EBIITONG passes.

EBIITONG   Ka-paa-wiijiwin wii-gkendmaa ezhchigeng paa-aashtoonigeng. [*You are not much older than me, and you've been trading for a long time. I'm going with you.*]

NIMKII   Baamaapii go gegii nendaagziyan ka-kwejmigoo. Ka-paa-kinoomaagoo. [*I am not you. When you are wanted, you'll be asked.*]

GCHI-GIMAA   Esnaa paa-mnowaabmewzin Nimkii. Bebaa-zhaayan gegwa zaam gbeying baa-ndenke. Gchi-zhaa'zhi eko-baabiiyag na'aangish. [*Prosper on this journey of yours, Nimke. And don't make this trip too long. I have waited a long time for a son.*]

NIMKII   (*to NGASHI*) Miigwech ezhi-mno-gnoozhyan. Naagdawenim maaba. [*Thanks for your good words. Take care of her.*]

NGASHI   Wiin sa go naa maaba nga-naagdawenmig. [*I'm an old fool now. She will take care of me.*]

NANGOONS   Gaa gwa gnigenh maaba daagii-maajaasiiba. [*He should not be going.*]

NGASHI   Oo! Da-bi-bskaabii nii maaba Nimkii. Enso-niibing sa nii maaba da-maamaajaa miidash dgwaagig ji-bi-giiwed. Niin gii-aapdendwiba ndanniim. Gaa'sh wii go wiikaa ndoo-nenmaasii. Nmakwenmaa jibwaa nbaa'aanh. Ndoo-ngamtoowaa. [*Your Nimke will return. Every summer he will leave you, and every autumn he'll come back. But my man is gone for good. Not from my heart; he'll always be there. Some nights, little Nohngose, when I lay down to sleep, I'm filled with such a longing for him. And I sing, with such a tiny voice, so no one will hear but him.*]

Wiijiwshin Nangoons. Epiichi-nokiiying ka-gchi-nbwaachidimi. [*Come and work beside me today, and we'll talk too much.*]

EBIITONG   Gaa geyaabi maanda wii-ntankamgizyaanh. Aabdig sa gwa wii-nokiiyaanh. Genii nii-waamdawen, nii-waabmigoo, mii go gegiinwaa ge gegiinwaa ge-zhichigeyegba. [*I have no time to waste on your games. I must work and prove myself. You should do the same.*]

CHI-GIMAANS   Aaniipiish ezhaayeg? [*Where are you going?*]

EBIITONG   Nii-paa-miigaazo-niniw. [*I am going to be a warrior.*] *(He exits.)*

CHI-GIMAANS   Gdaa-paa-wiijwaanaa na maaba? [*Should we go with him?*]

BIIDAABAN   Giiwnaadzi gsha maaba. [*No, he's crazy.*]

EBIITONG   Mii na giiyenh. Aangwaamzin ezhyan. Gaawii gwa wii-maamiikwaandizyaanh Ngoding gii-giizhgak ngii-nsaaba gchi-Windigo gaa-biindgonang. [*Is that so? Well, you should be careful of the words you say to me. I don't like to brag, but I was the one that killed the great Windigo that came into your tent.*]

BIIDAABAN   Nda-binoojiinwinaaba wi pii. Mii go zhiwi enaasmiyaanh gii-biidaasmigaabwid, aapji go mko-biiwye, mkomiinsi-shkiinzhigwe, gaagiinko-shkiinzhigwe, ndaa-ni-nesendaag. [*I was only a child at the time. It stood there in front of me, all hairy and cold. You could see the ice like blades coming from its eyes. It tried to breath on me.*]

ADDIK   Aanii dash gaa-zhichigeyan? [*What did you do?*]

BIIDAABAN   Gii-ntami-nesendwaan miish geyii gchi-Windigo gii-nkaan-mjishing. [*He breathed first and the Windigo fainted dead.*]

ADDIK   Daapnan maanda bezhig. [*Choose a stick.*]

DAANIS   Wenesh nendwendaman? Wenesh ge eyaad? [*What do you want? Who is with you?*]

CHI-GIMAANS   Zhigaag. [*A skunk.*]

BIIDAABAN   Aabji-biijmaagzi wa zhigaag. [*You can always smell where he is.*]

ADDIK   Mii sa gkenmag zaagi'id. [*Now I'm sure she's in love with me.*]

BIIDAABAN Zhigaagoons eta gashwan zaagigoon. [*Only a mother skunk loves the little skunk.*]

DAANIS Nbiijmaamaa sa go wa zhigaag. Besho gwa yaadig. Aaniipiish yaad? Oodi na? [*I can smell that skunk. He's close by. Where is he? Is he over there?*]

Nkwetwishin. Nmoosh'aa go wiya maa yaad. Gaawii maamdaa wii-paa-yaayan. Bekaa naaniibwin. Mii go eta waa-zhi-mkawnaa. Gaawiin wi-ikaa miinwaa gdaa-wiidookoosnoo. [*Somebody has to answer me. Someone is moving. You are supposed to keep still until I find you. I will never play with you again.*]

EBIITONG says…"Kwezens"… as action shifts from the group.

MA'IINGAN Miigaazo-niniins gbi-zhaa maanpii nwanj wii-mno-wiis-niyaanh. [*You come to give me a greater feast, little warrior.*]

EBIITONG Giishpin nendman wii-bmaadziyan, ka-ni-maajaa. [*If you want to live, go away.*]

MA'IINGAN Gitchi-mshkawtaagos gwa miigaazo-niniins. Gaawiin ngoji nii-zhaasii. Maanda ge gii-waabmiyan mii go wii-nboyan. [*See how bravely the little warrior speaks. I will not go away. Now that you have seen me, you will die.*]

EBIITONG Ka-miigaanin gwa. Giishpin gwa maanzhtowaanh nga-wiindmawaag nwiiji-nishnaabemog maanda niniiyaanh. [*I will fight you. If I am victorious, then my people will know I am a man, and I will ask pardon for taking your life.*]

MA'IINGAN Gaagiigdan gwa miigaazo-niniins. Mii gwa aapji shkwaaj wii-giigdoyan. [*Speak more, little warrior. These words will be your last.*]

EBIITONG Giishpin sa wii-nshiyan, maaba nshiimenh ka-shkonnaa. [*If you kill me, wolf, then spare my little sister.*]

MA'IINGAN Giishpin sa bwaa-gshkozid jibwaa niisiigwandaagonebininaa, nga-shkonnaa. [*If she does not wake before I rip your throat, then she will be spared.*]

EBIITONG Aahaaw. Mii go wi. [*So be it.*]

Scene shifts.

MDIMOOYENH Mii eshkiniigaans gii-ziigsenig miskwiim gidkamig. Jibwaa shkwaa-niibing mskwi da-ziigjiwan. [*The blood of this child has spilled onto the earth. Before the end of summer this island will be a river of blood.*]

LUPI Nookmis, aanii dash maaba kwezens? [*Grandmother, what about this girl?*]

MDIMOOYENH   Nshin! [*Kill her!*]

LUPI   Nmanaadendaan gaa-naaknigeyaanh, gaa maamdaa, ni-soongon. [*I am honour-bound to spare her life.*]

MDIMOOYENH   Gmanaadendaan naaknigewin, gchi-zhaa'zhi gii-nbomgadiba wi. Nshin!   [*Honour is dead and gone from the world.*]

Scene shifts.

NGASHI   Nsayenh! Gaawii maamdaa maanda ji-nendmamba ngwisenh ji-gii-zhichiged. Nishke maaba dengwaang bmi-zhikozod miinwaa gondaagan ezhnaagdinig. [*You cannot think that this is the work of my son. Brother! Look at the wounds on the face and throat of this child.*]

GCHI-GIMAA   Gaawii maanda ndibaaknaziin, nishke maanda, miinwaa 'nishin maaba gwiizens. Maage gaa-nbogwenh... [*I make no judgments, but see here. The boy has disappeared. Either he is dead...*]

NGASHI   Gaawii ndebwe'endzii ji-gii-nbod ngwisenh. [*My son is not dead.*]

GCHI-GIMAA   Gchi-zhaa'zhi gaa-ko-maamnanenmag aanii waa-ni-naadzid. Ntaamaanzhendam. Wiiji-shkinwen wiidookwaad mii go eta wii-bmi-nda-miigaazod dbishko gwa naa daa-mooshkneshkaagwan wii-nshiwed. [*For some time I have seen a darkness growing in his spirit. We have brought peace to our village. Of all the young men, he most seeks battle. The hunger for killing is like madness within him.*]

NGASHI   Gaayii zhiwebsinoo wi. Gegii ngoding gaa-zhiyaayan, nsayenh, gegii ngoding kii-miskwii-ninjii. [*That is not true. You look at him and see yourself. The blood of others once washed over your hands, brother.*]

GCHI-GIMAA   Gaayii nii-dbaaknaasii. Baamaa pii gwa gii-mkawind mii geyii jj-giigdod. Ezhi-niizhyeg'sh ka-maajaam ji-baa-ndanegeyeg. Gaayii gwa ka-baa-nshike'zisiim. Gaayii gkendaaksinoo waa-ni-zhiwebak nongwa naagshig. [*I will not judge him until he has been found and can speak for himself. You two will join the search. Stay close together. We don't know what is in this night.*]

The group sets out to look for EBIITONG.

NGASHI   Aaniipiish yaayan ngwisenh? Gnoondoon gwa. Kii-gkenmin besho yaayan. Gwisin na enji-zaagiyeswan? Maajaan ndanniisim jibwaa gwendang maaba gashi. Giishpin zaagiyan... (*hums lullaby*) ...Gmak-wendaan na kwa gii-ngamtoonaa? [*Where are you, son? I hear your voice and I know you are near to me. Are you afraid of me? Is that why you don't show yourself? Come, my little man, before your old mother's heart breaks. See, how I sing the lullaby I used to sing. Remember?*] Enji-gaazootwiyan? [*Why do you hide from me?*]

EBIITONG *(voice-over)* Aapji gwa besho nda'aa ngashi. [*I am very close to you, Mother.*]

NGASHI Aabiish? Waamishin. [*But where, child? Show me where you are.*]

EBIITONG *(voice-over)* Ka-gchi-nendam pii waabmiyan mnik giigoon'ig gaa'debnagwaa. [*You will be proud of me when you see how many fish I have caught.*]

NGASHI Biizh, ka-gchi-waawiisnimi dash. [*Then bring them to me, and we will feast.*]

EBIITONG *(appearing before her)* Nashke maampii gwaabam ngashi. [*See, here I am, Mother.*]

NGASHI Gchi-miigwech debenjged bskaabwinad ngwisenh. Aaniipiish gii-yaayan niijaansenh. [*Thanks to the Creator for returning my son. Where have you been, child?*]

MDIMOOYENH appears.

MDIMOOYENH Nbowin kwii-biindgeshkaagnaawaa gdakiimwaang. [*There's death coming to your house.*]

NGASHI Gaawii booch gdaa-zegmisii aani-shkodetaagziyan. Aaniish gaa-doodwad ngwisenh? [*You are a ball of fire speaking words meant to frighten me. What have you done with my child?*]

MDIMOOYENH Yaa gwa oodi gsayenh gaa-zhi-naazhkowaad giwi niijaansag. [*He is where your brother sent all my children long ago.*]

NGASHI Mekomosen'ish, gdaa-ni-maajaa zhinda oodenaang. Gaa gegoo naabdasnoo gdoo-mashkiim. Gegoo ka-biindawendamaadzon mdimooyenzhish. Neyaab gdaa-biinaa niijaansenh. [*You smiling witch, haunt my village no more. Your medicine is bad and it will fall back on you. Evil thing, give me my boy.*]

MDIMOOYENH Kagwejim wii-zhawenminaa wiikaa yaamda'aaswin zhawendiwin. Gsayenh sa nii wa gaa-bi-nsaapa nwiidgemaagan, niijaansag miinwaa nwiidizhaanag maaba ge binoojiinh mii gwa zhiwi giji-shkodeng ezhi-mjigonaad ngii-gchi-noondaagos wii bwaa-bgijwebnaad zhiwi giji'iinh ezhi-gshkitoowaanh ngii-bgosenmaa wii-shkonnaad. [*You ask mercy from one who was shown no mercy. It was your brother who killed my husband and my children and my sisters and my brothers. He left only me, a woman who begged for her own life and the life of a grandchild. Your brother held this crying child over the flames of a fire.*]

NGASHI Gaa-zhi-bgosendman wii-shkonnind wa gooshenh, mii go ezhi-bgosenminaa bskaabwinad neyaab ngwisenh. [*You begged for the life of a child. Then I beg for the life of my son.*]

MDIMOOYENH   Kwe, gniijaanis zhaazhi gii-nbo. [*Woman, your child is already dead.*]

> *Scene shifts.*

ADDIK   Wegnesh ge wi byaabiitooyan? Nda'aa gwa zhinda. Nshike gego. Nshishin! [*Why do you wait? I am here. I am alone. Kill me!*]

LUPI   Aaniish gaa-namdaman wii-mkawyan enmamyan? [*How did you know where to find me? How do you know who I am?*]

ADDIK   Ngii-wiindmawewis. Mii go pii gaa-shkwaa nsad nwiijkiwenh miinwaa nshiimenh. [*My spirit knew you. Not long after you killed my best friend and his little sister.*]

LUPI   Ka-wiindmawewis maaba gwiizhenzhish gechi-piiknoowed. [*Such a big and ugly spirit for one who has big cheeks.*]

ADDIK   Aangwaamzin ezhnikaanad epiiknoowed, ngii-bi-zhaa zhinda wii-nsigoowaanh gaawii wii-baapnadaagoowaanh. [*Watch who you call fat-cheeks. I came here to be killed, not insulted.*]

LUPI   Nengaaj go ka-nsin. [*I'll kill you slowly, little idiot.*]

ADDIK   Gigiishtoon gwa. [*Just get it over with.*]

LUPI   Aaniish gwa enji-jaanmendaman wii-nboyan? [*What makes you hungry for death?*]

ADDIK   Niin sa ngii-wezhmaa wa kwezens. Gaa-shkwaa-giibiingwepzod, nshike gwa gii-yaa. Kina gwa ngii-bi-noopnangok. Mii gegii gii-bi-dgoshnan gii-bi-nsad. Ngoding go giizhgak ka-wiindmaag mnidoo aanii gaa-zhiwebak wi pii gaa-zhichigeyaanh bi-dbageyaanh bmaadziwin. Nshishin! [*I was the one who played the trick on DAANIS, and the others all followed me. We left her alone, her eyes blinded, to be caught and butchered by you. The great spirit will speak to you one day. For what I have done, I pay with my life. Kill me now!*]

LUPI   Daapnan gdinkaazwin wii-miigaazyan. [*Take up your weapon. Fight me for your life.*]

ADDIK   Zhaazhi kii-miinin maanda mookmaan. Giin gwa gdizhchige maanda. Booniikaw gonda bemaadzijig. [*I have given you my knife. The blade is broken. You have set the course. Prey on the people no more.*]

> *The group returns to the village.*

MDIMOOYENH   Gnawaabam maaba nooshenh, aapji gwa maaba megwaa mshkawzi. Enso-mwaad bemaadzinjin eshkam gwa mshkawzi. [*Look at my grandson now, how great and powerful he is. Each time he eats a human being he grows larger and larger and more fearsome.*]

GCHI-GIMAA Wenesh gegii waa-yaaman? [*What do you want?*]

MDIMOOYENH Nangoons.

GCHI-GIMAA Gaa go wenjizhid gdaawsii, gaa go wiikaa gdaa-miinsinoo maaba ndaanis. [*No, you are evil. I will never hand my daughter over to you.*]

LUPI Kina sa gwa iidig ge-mwagwaa bemaadzijig. Nangoons eta nga-shkonnaa. [*Then I will eat you and everyone else, until only Nohngose is left.*]

MDIMOOYENH Nga-baabiitoon ge-naaknige'endaman. Gaawii go gbeying. [*I will wait for your decision. But I won't wait long.*]

> *GCHI-GIMAA spots ZHASHK.*

GCHI-GIMAA Nwiijkiwenh, gchi-wiikaa kiigid. Wenesh naa waa-wiindmawyan? Aaniish naa ezhi-maanzhtowaanh? [*My friend, you rarely speak. Have you come to tell me how we conquer this enemy?*]

ZHASHK *(voice-over)* Ni-maajaan zhinda mnising. [*Leave this island.*]

GCHI-GIMAA Gaawii maamdaa wiiganii ji-aawyaangba. [*We would be cowards.*]

ZHASHK *(voice-over)* Gaa go gegoo tesnoo waa-zhi-bkinaageyan. [*There is no way to win.*]

GCHI-GIMAA Zhashk, booch sa gwa maaba ma'iingan nga-ni-noopnangonaa. [*Still, mighty crane, the wolf will follow us.*]

ZHASHK *(voice-over)* Giishpin nbiing ni-zhaad, wii-jaagzo. [*If he goes into the water, he will burn.*]

GCHI-GIMAA Aaniish ge wa waa-zhi-jaagzod nbiing? [*How can the water burn him?*]

ZHASHK *(voice-over)* Ngii-bgosenmaanaa debenjged wii-tood mshkawzi-win gaataa-mnis wii-naadmaagooyeg. Gchi-dago da-bi-yaa wii-gwaash-mineg. [*We have asked the Creator to place his power into the waters surrounding your island to protect you from this evil. Within the great wave that carries you to safe shores is the all consuming fire.*]

GCHI-GIMAA Weweni ngii-bzindam. Aabdig kwii-maajaami zhinda. Kina'sh go ka-maajiidoonaa ezhi-daniiying jibwaa bi-dgoshing maaba nini-ma'iingan waa-bnaaji'nang. [*I have listened. I know what must be done. We must rise up, pack what belongings we can take, and leave here before the man-wolf destroys us all.*]

CHI-GIMAANS Gda-kiimnaa gshii maanda. [*This is our land.*]

GCHI-GIMAA Gaa gwa maamdaa. Aabdig gwa kwii-aapji-maajaami. [*We must leave forever.*]

NANGOONS   Aaniipii dash maaba Nimkii waa-bi-zhi-giiwed. Gaa wiya da-yaasii. [*Who will Nimke have to come home to?*]

GCHI-GIMAA   Gnoodmaageninwag da-nonkiiwag wi. Wewiibtaag, aabdig kwii-maajaami. [*Our messengers will find him. We must leave quickly.*]

      Everyone assembles and prepares to leave.

BIIDAABAN   Baabiwshig! Gaa zhinda nshike nii-yaasii. [*Wait! Stay with me. I don't want to stay alone.*]

NANGOONS   Wewiibtaan! Aabdig wewiib kwii-dgoshnomi jiigbiig. [*Hurry! We have to get to the shore!*]

BIIDAABAN   Nii-waaskonetmawaa wa dibino gaa-ni-zhaagwenh wa gwiizhenzhish, da-'nishin, naadmawshin. [*I want to light a fire for ADDIK. Wherever he is, my silly boy, he will be lost without a fire to light his way. Help me.*]

      BIIDAABAN lights a fire.

Gzhiikaan gegii dbi'iidig ezhaawne. [*Travel with speed, my friend.*]

NANGOONS   Wewiibaan, maajaan. Aaniipiish iidig maaba nda-kwegaans gaa-miingoowaambaa. Gaawii zhinda tesnoo. Aaniipiish iidig. [*Come, we must hurry. My wampum necklace? It's not here. It's not here.*]

      MA'IINGAN enters.

MA'IINGAN   Nangoons, aaniipiish ezhaayan? [*Nohngose, where are you off to?*]

NANGOONS   Gaawii ngii-gkendziin. [*I don't know.*]

MA'IINGAN   Gegwa ngoji maajaake. Wiijgendwishin. Ka-naagdawenmin. [*Do not leave. Stay here with me. I will protect you.*]

NANGOONS   Gaawiin kii-gkenmisnoo. [*I don't know you.*]

MA'IINGAN   Giishpin aanwaabmiyan nga-gshkitoon wii-maandaawnini-iyaanh. [*If you do not like me I will change my looks. I can be more handsome than this.*]

LUPI   Gegwa bgidnishiike. Kina go gegoo gaa-zhi-mkweminaa da-nbomgad. [*Don't leave me here. All my dreams die with you.*]

NANGOONS   Nimkii nzaagaa. [*I love you, Nimke.*]

NIMKII   Bgidin maaba kwezens. [*Let her go.*]

MDIMOOYENH   Miigwemba wa Nangoons, daagii-bmaadzi gwa. Naaknigewin go eta ngii-biidoonaa. Kii-gchi-menshi'mi dash. [*If you had given him Nohngose, your daughter would still be alive. To repay you for the slaughter of my village, I asked only for Nohngose for my grandson. I offered all that I had, and you disgraced us.*]

GCHI-GIMAA   Gaansidam gaa-bi-zhiyaayaang gii-shkiniigyaang. Bjiinag nongwa gnasdoowenmin. Maaba gooshenh ndaagii-miigaadwimnaaba gaa dash go zhinaagsinoo, gaawii geyaabi wiya gwiiji-nishnaabem-naanig bmaadzisiiwag. [*My wrongs were the folly of youth. I know you now. Your son and I would compete, and fight, until it was either the death of your people or the death of mine.*]

MDIMOOYENH   Weweni go kii-dbage. Washme ge gwa. Maaba miinwaa niin nii-dkonaanaa maanda mnis, kina go gegoo eteg. Debseg go mnik gaa-bi-zhi-nigaazyaang. Gdaa-ni-maajaa. Wiiba go naa maaba da-bgam-naandam. [*Still, see how you have paid? And more. My grandson and I claim your land and all that is on it. Leave. We are used to wounds, this boy and I. It won't be long before he hungers for your flesh.*]

GCHI-GIMAA   Nga-zhiitaasdoonan jiimaanan gondag jiibyensag ji-bi-waad, maaba ndaanis miinwaa na'aangish. Nga-ni-maajiinaag dash. [*I will prepare the boats for the bodies of my daughter and my son and I will take them from here. Do not deny me that.*]

MDIMOOYENH   Ni-maajaan. [*Go.*]

Aaniish mii sa ji-boonendamang. Aabdig sa gwa geyaabi bezhig kwe yaadig ge-wiidgemad oodenaw ji-zhitooweg. Gaa ge wiya ka-bi-gbanni-goosiiyaa. Maampii mshkiki nga-toon ji-ni-mno-zhiyaayan. Gegwa zegzike. Maanda shkode ka-naadmaagwan ji-ni-mno-zhiyaayan, ji-ni-mno-bmaadziyan. Aaniish gwa naa ezhnaagok niwi gshkiinzhigoon. Gegwa gnawaamizhiike. Ngoji oodi naabin. [*See now, we'll ease the pain, my grandson. There is another bride for you somewhere, you'll see. And we will bring her back and make a village that no man will burn down. See boy, I light the fire to make you my own sweet one again. See, now the medicine is in the flames to make you well and strong. Don't be afraid. The fire is life to you. My medicine is strong. I don't know those eyes. Turn them away from me. Turn them away from me.*]

LUPI   Mdimooyenh, gii-nishin gwa gegeti wi gmashkiim miinwaa kii-naadmaagnaa, kii-zhjaabwingonaa. Nashke dash gaa-zhichigeyan gaa-zhi-naabjitooyan. Gaa gwa geyaabi giiwsenini ndaawsii. Ngiiwsendowaag bemaadzijig. Gaa gsha gwa wiya geyaabi bemaadzid wii-dkokiid zhinda mnising. Niin gweta zhinda nii-yaa. Gaa ge gwa wiikaa nii-maajaasii. Mii gwa zhinda wii-aabji-dnizyaanh. [*This is how I will be. Always. Your medicine power was strong and saved us once but look how you've used it, old woman. Look how you've used me. What spirit is left within me fit for a bride to love and cherish? I am a hunter of people. But they are safe from me. No living thing will set foot on this island while I am here. And I know I will never leave.*]

MDIMOOYENH   Maanoo nii gwa naa gdaa-naagdawenmin. Gaa gwa gbeying nii-yaasii. [*My time is not long. Let me care for you.*]

LUPI Pii gwa bkadeyaanh gaa gwa gnigenh gmashkiim wi piichi'iimgasnoo wii-naadmawyan nwanj da-nishin ji-maajaayan. [*Your medicine is not strong enough to protect you from me. With time, my hunger will grow.*]

MDIMOOYENH Gmaajiinaashkaw maampii mnising. Giishpin maajiinaashkawyan mkwenim maaba mdimooyenh. Gichi-piitenmin kii-gchi-nenmin. Biinash ni-nbowaanh ka-kinoodamoon ji-ni-mno-bmaadziyan, ji-ni-mno-zhiyaayan. [*Listen. And hear me. If you drive me from this island, hear me. I thought the punishment for what I'd done would be mine alone. I never meant to hurt you. I love you, child. Remember always. This old woman loves you and will die with a prayer for your safe return on her lips.*]

LUPI Eshki-dgoshnaa zhinda mnising gii-minwendaagwad. Kina gegoo ngii-noondaan, bemaadzijig baapwaad. Nongwa dash nboodewad. Nbo-mnis nongwa maanda aawan. Nangoons miinwaa Nimkii ndebtawaag. Giizowi nongwa Nimkii. Geyish dbik-giizowi Nangoons. Kaagige zaagidwag nongwa. Bsagiishbikak'sh genii nda'aa megwe nbowin. [*The night I first set foot on this island, I heard the sounds of living. Laughter. Now it is a lonely place. I live on an island of death. That is Nohngose and Nimke. He is the sun. She is the moon. Their love is eternal. I am lost in the false dawn between them. Forever.*]

The end.

Glossary

aankanootmaage	he/she interprets
aashtoonge	no trade
bemaadzid	person (human being)
bemaadzijig	persons (human beings)
binojiinyag	children
binoojiinh	child
bmaadzi	he/she is alive
bmaadziwag	they are alive
bmaadziwin	life
dago	wave
dagowesing	waving waters
da-ni-bmaadziwag	they will live on
danniiman	his men
dansan	his/her daughter
dbikak	at night
dbik-giizis	moon
dbikong	last night
dnizi	he/she stays there
dnizwag	they stay there
eko-binoojiinwiying	since we were children
gaa wiikaa nginwaabmigsii	she never looks at me
gaa wiikaa	never
gaawii gdaa-zegmisii	you cannot frighten me
gaawii gii-biidoosiin	he did not bring it
gaawii nginwaabmigsii	she is not looking at me
gaawii nzegzisii	I am not afraid
gaawii/gaayii/gaa	no (negative form "not")
gbiidoon	you bring it
gbiinaa	you bring it
gdaanis/gdaansenh	your daughter
gdizhtwaaninaa	our belief/our tradition
gii-nbo	he died
giishpin/iishpin	if
giizis	sun
gwiizens	boy
gwiizensag	boys
gzaagaa	You love her/him

gzaagin	I love you
jiigbiig	near the shore
ka-waabmigoo	we will see you
kinwaabmig	she/he is looking at you
koos	your father
kwe	woman
kweng	as a woman
kwewag	women
kwezens	girl
kwezensag	girls
ma'iingan	wolf
ma'iingni-ndib	wolf's head
ma'iingniyaanan	wolf's skins
maaba	this (living)
Maajaan!	come!
maanda	this (not living)
miigaazo	he/she is fighting
miigaazo-nini	warrior
miigaazo-niniins	little warrior
mnis	island
mnishensing	on the small island
mnising	small island
mshkiki	medicine
na'aangish	my son-in-law
naagshig	in the evening
naaknigewin	decision/law/proposal
naaniimi	he/she keeps dancing
nashenh	my aunt
nbiidoon	I bring it (classified not living)
nbiinaa	I bring it (classified as living)
nbiish	water
nbowin	death
nda-aankanootmawaa	I am interpreting for him/her
ndaanis/ndaansenh	my daughter
ndanniim	my man
ndanniisim	my little man
ndib	head
ngamo	he/she sings
ngamwag	they are singing
ngashi	my mother

nginwaabmig	she is looking at me
ngwis/ngwisenh	my son
nigaazi	he/she is poor
niibwi	he/she is getting married
niijaansag	my children
niijaansenh	my child
niimi	he/she is dancing
niimwag	they are dancing
nini	man
ninwag	men
nongwa	today, (now)
nookmis	my grandmother
noos	my father
nooshenh	my grandson
nsayenh	my brother (eldest)
nshiimenh	my younger brother/sister
nwiijkiwendig	my friends
nwiijkiwenh	my friend
nzaagaa	I love her/him
oosan	his/her father
shkiinzhgoon	eyes
shkiinzhig	eye
shkode	fire
waab	to see
wiidgemaagan	spouse
wii-niibwitwaad/wii-wiidgoowaad	that he will marry her
zaagidwag	they love each other
zaagidwin	love
zegzi	he/she is afraid
zhaa	he/she is going
zhaazhi gii-nbo	he is already dead
zhichige	he/she does something
zhigaag	skunk
zhigaagoons	little skunk
zhitwaawin	belief/tradition

New World Brave

Production Notes

New World Brave must be considered a seminal performance in De-ba-jeh-mu-jig's history of productions, for many reasons. It was the first time that the Four Directions Creation Process (4D) was utilized completely in the creation of a performance. The 4D Creation Process is a culturally and socially specific process, wholistic in nature; it recognizes the artist as the creation and the performance as the celebration. It recognizes that, as humans, we create with our entire being—our physical, our emotional, our intellectual, and our spiritual selves, and therefore it accepts and specifically supports the artist in all four of these areas. It is adapted to the skills and intuitions of artists who have been strongly influenced by the oral tradition; it is a process that nurtures honesty more than accuracy, and sharing more than starring. It is a process that consciously uses personal resources (physical—like a skill, emotional—a memory, spiritual—an experience, or intellectual—like an object) as the key to personal and group creation. The four main components of the 4D Creation Process are Clown, Improvisational Theatre, R.S.V.P. Cycle, and Neuro-Linguistic Programming.

After being performed at the Holy Cross Mission Ruins in Wikwemikong for De-ba-jeh-mu-jig's 2001 Mainstage production, the piece was further developed to tour the James Bay coastline. As you will see in this version of the script, a lot of the scenes were left open-ended in order to integrate the youths' own voices and experiences as a way for them to see their own lives and their own stories reflected on stage.

At times the actors in the show are playing "themselves" offering personal statements about their own views of the future and their place in it and at other times the actors are playing fictional characters.

New World Brave was collectively created by De-ba-jeh-mu-jig Theatre Group.

New World Brave was first produced in 2000 by De-ba-jeh-mu-jig Theatre Group, with the following company:

CLETIS	Cameron Courtorielle
JAAL	Raistlen Jones
YOZO	Bruce Naokwegijig
CHIEF	Joe Osawabine
CLEM	Chris Wemigwans

Directors:	David Skelton
	John Turner
Stage Management:	Jeffery Trudeau
Lighting Design:	Andy Moro
Sound Design:	Marc Nadjiwan
Set Design:	Moses Beaver
Costume Design:	Christine Williston

Characters

ACT I

CHIEF
YOZO
CLEM
CLETIS
JAAL

ACT II

CARL—Our main character has never been off of the reserve before but wants to move to the city to find a career in photography.
FRANK—An elder, CARL's uncle, and advisor.
DARIUS—A gang member; lived in the city most of his life and is thinking maybe it's time to go "home."
KENNY—DARIUS's older brother who introduced him to gang life.
CHIEF—The gang leader.
EBB—Another gang member.
BUM—A homeless man, whom CARL unintentionally befriends on the street.
COP #1—Has had plenty of dealings with the gang.
COP #2—Has had plenty of dealings with the gang.
NUTBAR—CARL's spirit guide.

New World Brave

ACT I

Act I is performed in the style of Pochinko Clowning or "Canadian Clowning" as it has come to be known, and is a bit of a parody of Act II. In this style of clown there is no "fourth wall" as in many other traditional theatre conventions, and the actors are responsive to the audience. Also there were no "scripted" lines; therefore we have provided the beats of the action to give you a sense of the scene.

Each of the characters, dressed as stage crew, is setting the stage for the De-ba-jeh-mu-jig performance of New World Brave.

They are unaware of the audience at first, but as soon as they become aware of the audience they quickly finish the set up.

CHIEF, the "crew boss," introduces "De-ba-jeh-mu-jig Theatre Group" to the audience.

No one comes out.

CHIEF re-introduces De-ba-jeh-mu-jig Theatre Group in hopes that they will appear.

Still no one comes out.

He begins to panic, as it seems that De-ba-jeh-mu-jig has not yet arrived.

He calls out the rest of the stage crew to find out who arranged for De-ba-jeh-mu-jig's arrival.

Everybody thinks it was everybody else's responsibility.

They quickly decide that the show must go on and they prepare to do the show themselves; they run backstage.

They come out each carrying a steel briefcase; they stand at specific spots around the stage and introduce themselves one at a time to the audience. As each introduces himself, he steps forward to the front of the stage and places his briefcase down where it sits for the rest of the act.

After introductions they all look to each other, not exactly knowing what comes next; CHIEF pulls out a script and then yells "Props!"

Somebody goes and gets the prop box, which is filled with costumes as well.

Each character pulls out a costume from the box.

The costumes are stereotypical Indian getups.

The Noble Savage.
Chicago Blackhawks' jersey.
Gang Member/Street Thug.
The Drunken Indian.
The Breach Cloth Warrior.
They examine each other and try to figure out who they are supposed to be.

The Noble Savage steps forward stoically and gives a Hollywood-esque "How"; everybody laughs.

The Chicago Blackhawk steps forward in his jersey and everybody does the "Tomahawk Chop" and chant—as happens at many Chicago Blackhawks' games to this day.

The Gang Member steps forward and pulls a gun on everybody.

The Drunken Indian steps forward and almost falls over hiccupping; again everybody laughs.

The Breach Cloth Warrior steps forward and lets out a war cry, again Hollywood-esque—boo boo boo boo.

Everybody laughs.

We come to another point of confusion as to what comes next in "the show."

CHIEF looks at the script again; meanwhile the others are looking into the prop box, and they find that there are still "props" in there so they each grab one. Each pulls out a cardboard square which on one side has a "Q" and on the other side "?" except for JAAL who pulls out a card with an "A" and "!."

They are all trying to figure out what it means until YOZO finally holds the question mark over his head and goes "Huh?"

The group then realizes that they all have "Questions" and that only JAAL has an "Answer" so they all begin to close in on JAAL, who takes off and a chase scene ensues. Throughout the chase scene the person being chased with the "Answer" keeps changing until the audience no longer knows who holds it.

At the end of the chase scene everybody collides into each other and the questions are scattered all over the stage with everyone scrambling to find the answer.

"Noweenagun" by Nadjiwan begins; everybody rises to their feet and makes their way to their steel briefcases which are situated at the front of the stage.

At this point, JAAL goes to get a garbage can and throws in his stereotypical get up. He then goes to each of the other characters who each, in turn, throw their stereotypes into the garbage can.

They then begin to take off their whiteface on stage in front of the audience.

Poster design by Ron Berti.

ACT II

Personal Introductions—I am...

> *These should be personal statements written by the performers based on how they see the future and what they see their role is. Example as follows:*

JOE   I am Joe Osawabine. I am Odawa from the Wikwemikong Unceded Indian Reserve. When we first came together to create this show we agreed upon a central theme. To tell the truth of our reality to create a change. I believe that one of the truths of all our realities is our ability to choose between yes and no. I know I may not always make the best choices and sometimes I find myself making the same bad choices over and over again. I believe that in order to move forward in a good way, we must learn from our past. Not to dwell in the past but to simply let our past inspire and inform our future. As we are young we have to look to our future. We have to be brave.

Seven Questions

What happened seven generations ago?

Seven years ago?

Seven months ago?

Seven days ago?

Seven hours ago?

Seven minutes ago?

Seven seconds ago?

Bush Party

> *CARL's friends (youth participants) are hanging out in the bush having a party, waiting for CARL's arrival while discussing the possibilities of what they could do for the evening and what CARL is up to and whether or not he is going to the city, and how they personally feel about leaving the reserve and moving to an urban centre.*

> *CARL enters carrying his camera; they greet him and offer him a beer and soon they decide to play the Inuit "hitting game" that a friend from Baffin Island has taught them. As they play they become drunker and drunker.*

The game consists of hitting each other on the shoulder, back and forth, harder and harder until somebody gives up.

One of the friends begins to play with CARL's camera. They begin to toss it around as they tease CARL. Finally it gets tossed extremely high into the air. As it is going up all the friends exit as quickly as possible leaving CARL onstage alone with his camera.

CARL   (*to himself*) That's it man; I've made up my mind. Nobody gives a shit around here.

Pictographs/Petroglyphs

Pictographs are rock paintings that have been left by our ancestors as a way to pass on traditional knowledge. Petroglyphs serve the same purpose but have been "carved in stone." Each participant will, in essence, become representations of the Pictographs/Petroglyphs. To come up with the Pictographs/Petroglyphs use the following process:

As a group, first identify the importance of the transmission of knowledge from our ancestors through the Pictographs and/or Petroglyphs, and what their relevance is in today's society.

Then, again as a group, explore the concepts of Searching, Receiving, and Giving and what that may mean to the group as a whole.

Each participant should then individually explore the concepts of Searching, Receiving, and Giving, and in doing so create three physical images that represent each concept utilizing their whole bodies.

Each participant should now have a total of nine physical/tableau images.

Each participant should now take their nine tableau images and find the best way for them to move from one tableau into the next in a continuous motion creating a movement piece.

Each participant could then present back to the group their Pictograph/Petroglyphs movement piece.

Have the participants perform their individual movement pieces simultaneously set to appropriate music at this point of the performance.

The Meeting—*The Rez*

> FRANK *is sitting by the fire.* NUTBAR *(a spirit) is also present but remains unseen by* CARL *in the following scene.* CARL *enters carrying a coffee and hands it to* FRANK.

FRANK   Aaniish enkamagak, Carl? [*What's going on, Carl?*]

CARL   Nothing. That's just it. I'm going to the city

FRANK   Mmmm, aaniidash? [*Why?*]

CARL   I just want to

FRANK   Miigowe wenjishing. Bemaadzijig nishnoog kchi-odenang Mii-na we'yaaman? [*That's a good reason. People get lost in the city. Is that what you want?*]

CARL   People get lost everywhere. I know what I'm doing.

FRANK   Wiidmoshin, gakiikenziin enookiyan. Aaniish e'na naakina ge yin? [*Tell me then. I don't know what you're doing. What's your plan?*]

CARL   I've applied to college in the city, and I've got a good chance of getting in. It could be more.

FRANK   Aaniish enji skoonwii'in? [*What are you going to school for?*]

CARL   Photography.

FRANK   Pho-tah-graphy. Just push the button; you can't do that here?

CARL   I could make a living maybe, pictures for calendars, newspapers…

FRANK   Zhoonyaa!! [*Money!!*]

CARL   It's not just about money. I think it could be helpful for our people.

FRANK   Doopwaasing waa-tatek mzinigan gwii-saak mzinaazwinak wi aazhibikong gaa-zhi-miiznaabkage yaad nishinaabek mzinaadek. [*You want to put pictures of what the Indian carved into the rocks in a book, that's going to lie around on a little table?*]

CARL   I mean why not? We use tape recorders to preserve our language; what's the difference…?

FRANK   Gegwaa!! Gii-kinomoon wii-mnaadendmaa gegoo, ngii-nendam. [*Don't! I thought I taught you about respect.*]

CARL   I do respect you. That's why I had to tell you.

> *A moment of silence*

FRANK   Carl?

> FRANK *tosses* CARL *a pendant.*

CARL (*reading pendant*) Heal the circle that was broken, and you'll find your wounds will mend.

FRANK Mmmm.

CARL Heal the circle that was broken and you'll find your wounds will mend…

> *CARL exits and FRANK sends NUTBAR off with him. He remains with CARL, but still unseen by him, pretty much throughout the rest of the show, acting as a spirit guide.*

Wagon Burners

> *Rap song performed by the cast.*

Wagon Burners uneducated punks
Scalpers and braves homeless Indian drunks
The sea of labels in which we drown
Own them first they'll never bring us down
Wounded Knee, Ipperwash, The Trail of Tears
Through the ages living in fear

Anna Mae Aquash was shot down
Cuz she worked for AIM and she stood our ground
Little Miss Aquash life cut short
FBI—AIM who do you support
Power to the people Red skins forever
Fighting for our rights and her hands were severed

We've been hurting and drinkin' away our depression
From five hundred years under suppression
Time to quit our cryin'
Time to stop our dyin'
We ain't got the time to pay for the crime
Keep alive stand up strong
With these five words we can't go wrong

Five little Indians from across the land
Coming together trying to make a stand
We came from different worlds it seems
Never too late to change our destiny

Wagon Burners uneducated punks
Scalpers and braves homeless Indian drunks
The sea of labels in which we drown
Own them first they'll never bring us down

Wounded Knee Ipperwash, The Trail of Tears
Through the ages living in fear

Leonard Peltier's unruly conviction
For a crime he didn't do he's living in restriction
C'mon man just let him go
He didn't do it now we all know
Our people lived free oh can't you see
Keepers of the earth that's our destiny

We've been hurting and drinkin' away our depression
From five hundred years under suppression
Time to quit our cryin'
Time to stop our dyin'
We ain't got the time to pay for the crime
Keep alive stand up strong
With these five words we can't go wrong

Five little Indians from across the land
Coming together trying to make a stand

Brothers—*The City*

> KENNY *is getting ready to head out to the gang meeting putting on his gang colors—i.e., a red bandana—and DARIUS is watering his cactus.*

KENNY   Come on man, let's go!

DARIUS   Wait let me finish this.

KENNY   It doesn't need water. It grows in the desert, for chrissakes. Come on, we're late.

DARIUS   So what, they're always late anyway! Fucking Indians running on Indian time.

KENNY   Weptan dimwezhish. [*Hurry up, old lady.*] *(seeing DARIUS's apprehension)* What's the problem?

DARIUS   Forget it.

KENNY   What?

DARIUS   I just don't feel like going today.

KENNY   *(mockingly)* I just don't feel like going today. Get over it!

DARIUS   Aren't you tired of this?

KENNY   What?

DARIUS   Living like this.

KENNY   Fuck you! Get your own place then.

DARIUS   I don't mean living here—all this shit we do!

KENNY   Who, us?

DARIUS   Yeah us! All of us! You, me, the boys, the gang.

KENNY   You chose this path Darius, with me. You know the rules. You're in for life. You can't just walk away. You leave and were both gonna turn up dead. These guys are our friends. Every single one of them would take a bullet for you. I would take a bullet for you. And you damn well better do the same for me, for us!

DARIUS   It's just about taking a bullet?

KENNY   You're just an Indian in the city. What else are you going to do?

DARIUS   We shouldn't have to die like this.

KENNY   Everybody dies. Like a warrior? Or a dog in a ditch!

> *KENNY leaves and DARIUS has a moment on stage alone and apprehensively follows.*

Gangland—*The City*

CHIEF   Here's the plan. We found B.J.'s family, Ebb. Gun?

> *EBB pulls the gun out from the front of his pants.*

Kenny?

> *EBB holds out the gun towards KENNY.*

KENNY   I think Darius wants this one, Chief.

CHIEF   Great.

EBB   Darius. *(hands gun to DARIUS)*

DARIUS   Piece of cake.

> *DARIUS cocks the gun dangerously, looking directly at KENNY, and exits stage left. KENNY watches him leave and has a look of genuine concern for his brother.*

EBB   What's up with him, you?

KENNY   Nothing, he's just worried about his prickly pear.

> *They all laugh and exit stage right, except for KENNY who stays looking in the direction of where DARIUS left.*

KENNY Hey you! Wait up!

> *KENNY follows the gang off.*

Brother Run

> *This scene is stylized to look like a music video using various lighting effects. It depicts CARL's journey to the city and DARIUS's attempt to evade the police after B.J. turns up dead. It is set to the song "Brother Run" by Nadjiwan.*

Listen to the ones, before you
Listen to what they have to say
Look to the ones before you
Look to them, to show you the way

Follow the path, left unspoken
Follow the path that will never end
Heal the circle that was broken
And you'll find your wounds will mend

Brother run from broken circles
Brother run under a wounded sky
Brother run look for your kind
Brother run until your wounds are dry

Listen to those distant voices
Listen to what they have to say
Hold on to your words and your choices
As only these can show you the way

Follow the path left unspoken
Follow the path from the past
To heal the circle that was once broken
Break free from this fast

The City

> *CARL arrives in the city for the first time. The city scene is set up using the participants and their personal pictographs that were established earlier; this time the pictographs represent the busy-ness of the city. Again this should be set to appropriate music, which is also representative of the city. The pictographs remain stationary and CARL is making his way through them as though he is making his way through crowded streets, being nudged and shoved every which way. CARL exits and the pictographs come to a slow halt.*

Rejection

> *CARL is at his apartment opening his mail, and notices a letter regarding his schooling application.*

CARL   *(excited)* Yes! Finally. *(reading)* Dear Mr. Oskineegish. That's me. Thank you for your portfolio and application... however... we regret to inform you... lack of experience... this is bullshit. Kicked out before I was even in. New record.

> *CARL looks at his camera and grabs it angrily and raises it high in the air as though to smash it on the ground. NUTBAR intervenes and stops him. CARL instead begins to vigorously clean the lens.*

Spirit Stealer

> *BUM is sleeping on the sidewalk. CARL passes by and notices him and begins to take pictures of him while he sleeps. BUM wakes up to the flash of the camera and quickly notices CARL.*

BUM   Hey, you! What, what, what are you doing?

CARL   I just wanted to take your picture.

BUM   Of this? This?

CARL   I didn't think you'd mind.

BUM   You don't know me!

CARL   I'm sorry.

BUM   Who wants to see a picture of this? Me? My family? Jean Chrétien?

CARL   I'd like to, okay?

BUM   Who are you? I don't know you.

CARL   Your situation...

BUM   Are you nuts? You think this is interesting? This is shit!

CARL   What? No. I wasn't...

BUM   Why?

> *Pause.*

You don't even know what you got. Do you?

CARL   It's just a camera.

BUM   Steal my spirit. You were going to show people who I am. Without my knowing.

CARL   I...

BUM   You were going to show people who I am.

CARL   But...

BUM   Without my knowing.

CARL   I'm sorry. Do you want the film?

BUM   Why should I care? You're just a cameraman. Showing everybody how it is. Go ahead. Take the picture.

CARL   No. It's all right.

BUM   Take the goddamn picture. This is how it is.

Carwash

> *DARIUS is on the street with a cardboard sign. He is advertising a charity carwash. CARL comes by and starts taking pictures of him.*

DARIUS   What the hell?

CARL   I'm just taking a picture.

DARIUS   I know people who would kill you for that! That's dangerous. Give me the film.

CARL   No. I can take pictures of whatever I want.

> *Two COPS enter and see the interaction between CARL and DARIUS.*

DARIUS   Hand it over!

CARL   The film is mine. *(noticing the COPS)* Hello, officers.

COP #1   Good afternoon, gentlemen.

DARIUS   Shit!

COP #2   Darius, what's all the commotion?

DARIUS   Nothing.

COP #2   *(to COP #1)* It looks like there's something going on.

CARL   I'm just taking some pictures.

COP #2   A tourist? Let's take a look at your film canisters.

DARIUS   I'm just setting up for the friendship centre carwash.

COP #1   The gang is turning to carwashes? Taking blood off the seats I suppose.

DARIUS   No. I'm not into that anymore.

COP #1   Ever heard of B.J.?

> *DARIUS is silent. CARL has started to take pictures of the interaction.*

Please come with us.

DARIUS   I'll have to get someone to take over here for me first.

COP #1   Now!

> *The COPS advance on DARIUS.*

DARIUS   Hey you can't touch me!

COP #2   This time, we can!

> *DARIUS attempts to flee. He uses his sign to fight them off. They wrestle him to the ground. CARL goes to run away, not wanting to get caught up in the scene, but NUTBAR intervenes and stops him from fleeing. CARL then takes out his camera and begins taking pictures of the whole altercation. COP # 1 notices CARL and the camera.*

COP #1   *(to COP #2)* Camera!

> *CARL flees.*

Chokecherry Lane

> *This scene depicts COP #1 and COP #2 severely beating DARIUS, and leaving him to die. It is stylized to look like frame-by-frame snapshots as seen through the lens of CARL's camera. It is set to appropriate music.*

Time To Go Home

> *This scene should be set to soothing music to set the tone. DARIUS is lying in a hospital bed. KENNY enters and sits by DARIUS's side, watching him in his coma. KENNY takes the gang colours— i.e., the red bandana—off of DARIUS as though to release him from the gang and ties it around his wrist and goes to leave the hospital.*

DARIUS   *(waking up)* Kenny.

KENNY   Darius! You're awake. I hate hospitals, man. I haven't been here since…

DARIUS   I know… Grandpa…. He came to me.

KENNY   What?

DARIUS   Grandpa came to me.... It seemed so real. I think it's time to go home. We can't die like this.

KENNY   Dying is easy.... We can't "live" like this. *(shows him the red bandana he had taken from him)*

> *They just have a moment together where DARIUS realizes that he is released from the gang but also knowing that KENNY will not be coming with him. Then KENNY exits. DARIUS goes and looks out the window down into the street where he sees the BUM sleeping with his hat on the ground in front of him. CARL comes walking by and places the pendant he had received from FRANK into the BUM's hat. The BUM wakes up and sees the pendant and reads it.*

BUM   "Heal the circle that was broken and you'll find your wounds will mend."

> *The BUM goes to place his hat on his head and for whatever reason decides not to place the hat on his head as the hat clearly marks his identity as a "bum." We should see a physical shift in his demeanour, leaving the audience to believe that he is going off to have a more meaningful experience.*

Courtroom

> *COP #1 and COP #2 stand on one side of the stage and DARIUS stands on the other side of the stage, alone.*

VOICE   *(off stage)* All rise!

> *JUDGE enters and stands centre stage between the two parties.*

(off stage) Court is now in session.

JUDGE   *(to DARIUS)* These are some pretty serious claims you are making towards the police department. And without substantial evidence to corroborate your story I'm afraid this court has no other choice but to find the defendants not guilty.

CARL   Wait!

> *COP #1 and COP #2 look at each other as CARL steps up to the bench.*

JUDGE   Who are you?

CARL   My name is Carl Oskineegish; I think I might have some evidence to support this man's claims. Pictures, Your Honour.

JUDGE Approach the bench.

> *JUDGE takes the folder and as he looks at the pictures we see the images from the earlier scene, "Chokecherry Lane," come to life again.*

In light of this new evidence, this court finds that there may be enough evidence to substantiate this claim, and orders that a full investigation take place immediately into the beating of Darius Gregory.

VOICE *(off stage)* Court is adjourned.

> *The two COPS stare CARL down and exit. DARIUS goes up to CARL and shakes his hand.*

Nutbar Reveals Himself

> *Back at CARL's apartment.*

NUTBAR Hey! Why did the chicken cross the road?

CARL Who are you?

NUTBAR I'm a Nutbar.

CARL I'm a Nutbar.

NUTBAR No kidding. What are you looking at?

CARL You.

NUTBAR Me? Look at me! Take a picture! Oooh look at me, I'm a photographer. How's the calendar business? How's your life plan?

CARL What plan? There is no plan?

NUTBAR Ouch that hurt. You know, the one you were talking to Frank about. You know, the school thing?

CARL How the hell do you know all this? Who are you?

NUTBAR I told you I'm a Nutbar. *(laughs)* How's the courtroom business?

CARL Get out of here!

NUTBAR Ever get mad over a few pictures of you.

CARL You don't know me!

NUTBAR Spirit stealer. Spirit stealer.

CARL It was just a bum!

> *NUTBAR motions and almost magically the BUM enters and replays the earlier interaction between CARL and himself.*

BUM   Hey, you! What, what are you doing? Of this? This? You don't know me! Who wants a picture of this? Me? My family? Jean Chrétien? Who are you? I don't know you. Are you nuts? You think this is interesting? Why? You don't even know what you've got, do you? Steal my spirit! You were going to show people who I am. Without me knowing. Why should I care? You're just a cameraman showing everybody how it is. Go ahead. Take the picture. Take the goddamn picture! This is how it is.

    The BUM exits.

NUTBAR   And Darius?

CARL   He was from a gang!

NUTBAR   Hello? Is anybody home? Why did you take the pictures in the first place?

CARL   There was something…

NUTBAR   What was it?

CARL   I don't know. It had me.

NUTBAR   It had you and you had to have it.

CARL   Yeah. It was right there in the lens. It was perfect.

NUTBAR   Did you capture it? Steal it? Twist it?

CARL   It was the right choice. Pictures don't lie. I had to do it. It was beautiful.

NUTBAR   What does Darius look like now?

CARL   He's a sign for us.

NUTBAR   And the bum?

CARL   Yes, him too.

NUTBAR   The cops got a slap on the wrist. And the bum is still sleeping on the streets.

CARL   The cops will think twice now.

NUTBAR   That's not much of a difference.

    NUTBAR exits leaving CARL on stage alone.

CARL   I honour those men. They are depending on me. Our songs. Our stories. We are the images we create. You will see it or you won't. I have my vision.

"Heritage" by Nadjiwan

The Power is given to us, try and use it well
Cherish what surrounds us, hold this land sacred
Know of our limitations, know of our place
In the circle

Lifeblood flows through these veins
Giving us all that we need
Providing us with sustenance
Satisfying our basic pleasures
Without you I cannot survive
Without you I have no home

Remember the tree of life and your soul spirit
See far and you shall fulfill your vision
Remember the tree of life and your soul spirit
See far and you shall fulfill your vision

Keep alive this wisdom
Keep alive this wisdom

Seven Questions

What will happen in seven seconds?

Seven minutes?

Seven hours?

Seven days?

Seven months?

Seven years?

Seven generations?

When I am...

When I am darkness, people will know the way.
When I am an idea, people will hear me.
When I am leaves, my children will still be here.
When I am forgotten, energy will follow through.
Because we are forgiving the past, we can move forward.

Chi-miigwech.

The end.

Ever! That Nanabush!

Ever! That Nanabush! is an adaptation of traditional stories as retold by Daphne Odjig-Beavon.

Ever! That Nanabush! was first produced in 2002 by De-ba-jeh-mu-jig Theatre Group, with the following company playing various characters:

Cameron Courtorielle
Ralph Courtorielle
Sharon King
Tammy Manitowabi
Elisha Sidlar
Chris Wemigwans

Director:	Bruce Naokwegijig
Stage Management:	David Osawabine
Set and Lighting:	Joe Osawabine
Costume Design:	Bill Shawanda

Glossary of Native words:

Mandamin	Corn
Nokomis	Grandmother
Amik	Beaver
Noodin	Wind
Biidaasige kwe	Sunlight Woman
Ahnii	Hello
Gaiashk	Seagull
Giigonh	Fish
Nahowdush	all right then

Characters

NANABUSH
CHORUS

The Animals:
RACCOON
RABBIT
BEAR
SQUIRREL
CHIPMUNK
FOX
DUCK # 1, 2, 3, 4
GOOSE # 1, 2, 3, 4
WEASEL
SKUNK
MUSKRAT
PORCUPINE
FISH
SEAGULL
DEER
TURTLE
INSECTS
BEAVER

The Immortals:
SNOW SPIRITS #1, #2
THE SPIRIT OF WINTER
NOODIN
FIRE
THE SPIRIT OF THUNDER
SUN
MANDOMIN
PINK
RED
BIRCH
SPRUCE

The Humans:
ISSIE
REGIS
NOKOMIS
MAN
WOMAN

Photo layout by Ron Berti. Design concepts by Bill Shawanda.

Ever! That Nanabush!

Nanabush and the Rabbit

Somewhere in some forest.

BEAR enters and begins to look for food, looking through an empty bag of garbage (which he is carrying with him).

RABBIT appears almost secretly from a different part of the stage and mischievously watches BEAR for a moment.

SQUIRREL enters and begins also to look for food, searches through BEAR's bag. BEAR obviously is very protective of it and growls at SQUIRREL.

SQUIRREL   I'm looking for some nuts. I left them here yesterday. Have you seen them?

BEAR   Nope.

SQUIRREL   They've round, hard shells. You have to use your teeth to crack them open, to eat the inside part. I love the inside part. You know which one is my favourite? Well I love them all, but the beechnut, by far is the best I've tried. It is so yummy, tasty, and delicious. Then there is the walnut. But I don't see too many walnuts around here. So I usually load up on acorns.

BEAR   I haven't seen any nuts around here. Or have I?

BEAR stares at SQUIRREL who is scampering, looking for the pile of nuts.

SQUIRREL   No. I'm just looking for a pile of nuts and I can't seem to find them anywhere. Yesterday, I did leave them here. I said to myself, I'm going to leave the nuts here, and be back tomorrow to get the rest.

BEAR   I don't really care for nuts of any kind, but if I do see any, I will tell you.

SQUIRREL   You are kind, Bear. Sometimes. But thank you. Oh look there! I see them now, over here.

SQUIRREL runs to the opposite side of the stage and inspects each nut carefully.

BEAR continues to look in his bag for food.

WEASEL enters with SKUNK, who is carrying a spray bottle filled with water.

WEASEL   No, no. I think you're wrong, and I would have to say that only because I don't agree with you.

SKUNK   No, you're not listening. I'm telling you, that is how they used to do it; now they use spears. I've seen it done before.

WEASEL   Why can't you just show me then? How hard is that?

SKUNK   What? Show you that? It's impossible. You know we'll get caught and wind up tomorrow's lunch or dinner.

WEASEL   Tah! Maybe me, but you? No, I don't think they care for you too much.

SKUNK   Oh you're nice! Real nice. Don't care about how that makes me feel right now. Nice. Just nice.

> *SKUNK sprays WEASEL with the spray bottle.*

WEASEL   Oh, why can't you just get over it? So you're not the desired one. Neither am I. Why can't you just get over that fact? I have and look at me!

> *WEASEL stands very proud as if to show off and SKUNK sprays him again.*

SKUNK   No. I am very worthy, I am extremely soft, and my fur is outs—

> *RABBIT who has been watching all this time comes racing in, making his presence known.*

RABBIT   You're not going to believe this! I just heard this! Wait! Let me catch my breath. Wait, wait, okay, okay, okay. I'm here. I just heard that Sun and Moon are never coming out again, and all will be dark forever! Forever, everything gone, or in total darkness. We must do something. You must tell all. I will go this way! Go! Go Weasel man, go Skunk, tell the animals whom we share this beautiful forest with.

> *WEASEL and SKUNK are startled and obey RABBIT. RABBIT then goes to BEAR, BEAR hollers and runs off. They all pass each other, some running off stage some running back on stage, sometimes bumping into one another.*

ALL ANIMALS   Darkness forever! The Sun and Moon will be gone! We must gather and get ready for this great catastrophe! Darkness for all eternity! We must be ready for this great catastrophe! We all must gather. There will be no Sun, no Moon! Dark forever!

> *SQUIRREL, CHIPMUNK, FOX, and MUSKRAT join the pandemonium. RABBIT sits offstage, perhaps in the audience, laughing at the chaos.*

CHORUS   Rabbit! What have you done? You have told these poor helpless souls a terrible lie. What has become of you, dear Rabbit? Rabbit! Where is your conscience? Have you any conscience? What will Nanabush, our great leader, think? What will the Sun and Moon think?

RABBIT   We all must take cover somewhere!

BEAR   We must gather, we must get enough food for all eternity. We must feed ourselves forever. We must!

WEASEL   Darkness forever? Darkness forever! Oh great Sun, I will miss you. Oh beautiful Moon, I will miss you too!

CHIPMUNK   What can we do to stop this inevitable catastrophe? How, how can we stop this? How?!

All the animals continue to frantically gather food and other things they think they might need.

SKUNK   It'll be all right, it'll be all right. Darkness, it's okay—

BEAR   Food, food for eternity, forever, we must—

FOX   I must tell my aunt. Does she know this? I will tell my cousin. He must know. How many have heard this? Who else do I need to tell? Does my great-uncle—

CHIPMUNK   Okay, get it together. Get it together. Move forward, that's what Doctor Moro said. Move forward; don't dwell in the past. Don't dwell—

MUSKRAT   I accept the darkness! I will live in darkness. I am brave. I am the Muskrat! I will live in this dark world forever!

NANABUSH enters.

CHORUS   Nanabush, see what you have come home to? The Rabbit has betrayed all of the animals of the forest. It is him. Look and see who has done evil to our world.

NANABUSH   Fox, what has happened since I've been gone? Why does everyone appear to have gone crazy?

FOX   My grandma. I must go and tell her. I will bring... *(noticing NANABUSH)* huh? Nanabush? I am so sorry. I cannot talk with you today. I have many things to do. I have to find my grandmother. She must know.

FOX runs off.

NANABUSH   Friend Muskrat, do tell me, what has gone on? What has been the word?

MUSKRAT   The change is here. I am willing. I will speak to you when the eyes have no fear, Nanabush.

MUSKRAT runs off stage away from NANABUSH. NANABUSH tries to grab him, and sees BEAR running past.

NANABUSH   Bear! Hear me! What has happened? You stop! Tell me. I will not let you go.

BEAR   Did you not hear of the great catastrophe, Nanabush? A prophecy of doom, of darkness. The Sun and the Moon will be gone forever! We all must gather food, for eternity, for without Sun and Moon there will be no crops, no berries, no plants!

NANABUSH   Who has told you this?

BEAR   The Skunk has told me this news... I think...

CHORUS   And the Chipmunk had told it to the Squirrel, and the Porcupine had told it to the Chipmunk, and the Fox had told it to the Muskrat, and the Muskrat had told it to the Weasel and the Weasel heard it from?

Everything comes to a complete stop and every animal turns to WEASEL to hear what he has to say.

WEASEL   I heard it from the Rabbit.

CHORUS   What will he do? Will he banish him from the forest? Poor Rabbit, it was just a silly lie.

NANABUSH   I will find him, I will. I will not stop until he is here. *(looking everywhere he can think of for RABBIT)* Rabbit!? Oh Rabbit?!

RABBIT, who is still in the audience watching, laughs with great joy until NANABUSH runs past him and then stops and runs back. NANABUSH grabs him by the ears. As he does so, RABBIT's ears grow and grow. RABBIT clearly does not enjoy this. NANABUSH throws him on stage. NANABUSH then goes to him and punches him in the mouth, splitting RABBIT's lip in the process. RABBIT, feeling timid now, shows his wounds and is feeling very nervous.

CHORUS   Nanabush, look at this animal. A rabbit with long ears, and a split lip? How will he survive the humiliation of this? Rabbit, what have you done to yourself? Let your long ears and your split lip remind you of the lie you told and how it almost destroyed your friends of the forest.

RABBIT dances in forgiveness.

Now Rabbit, live as you will, for years to come you will see more journeys. That is how our Rabbit is the way he is! Now continue for what is about to be foretold...

Nanabush Loses His Eyeballs

BEAVER enters and begins working downstage on his dam.

CHORUS   Grandfather Sun, tell us, what does this day bring? Tales of mischief? A story as old as the first Moon? We will be patient and wait for the day's gifts.

SQUIRREL enters.

SQUIRREL   Where are the seeds and acorns hiding today? The seeds and acorns?

CHORUS   This is where it unfolds. Gather. We invite you to share in this teaching.

SQUIRREL   Not a single seed. What about nuts? I hear nuts are good, seeds or nuts. Hmmm? Amik? Where does one look for seeds, nuts or acorns?

BEAVER   Have you tried Nanabush's garden? Many a treat can be salvaged there.

SQUIRREL   Thank you, my friend. The garden it is, to the garden!

CHORUS   Nanabush the great? Nanabush the wise? What will you do today? Frolic? Hunt? Or will you let what will be land on your lap? Grandfather Sun brings gentle goodness today, just listen. He beckons you to enjoy the day's bringings. Nanabush? Nanabush?!

NANABUSH enters yawning and stretching and kind of grumpy.

NANABUSH   Do you mind?! I was napping! Oh. *(acknowledging audience)* I'm sorry. Hmmm what shall I do today? Ask a winged one to tell me a story? Hmmm, maybe a swim with a finned one… I know! A good game with a four-legged one.

SQUIRREL   Is that you, Nanabush? I was on my way to go see you, I was. May I collect seeds and acorns in your garden? Or how about a nut or two? I hear nuts are good. May I?

NANABUSH   I don't see a problem. Gather what you will, but first how about a game of stone toss?

SQUIRREL   Oh Nanabush, the seeds and acorns and the one or two nuts cannot wait. I must prepare for the season's coming, Nanabush.

NANABUSH   I understand, my little brother. Go and prepare. I will find something to do.

SQUIRREL   Amik is at the river's edge. Perhaps he will partake in a game of stone toss with you.

CHORUS   Oh Nanabush, try your friend Beaver, playful in spirit, always up for an adventure of sorts. Follow the whacks! Follow the smacks! Follow your ears to what sounds like beckoning.

NANABUSH   Amik! Greetings, my dam friend. How does this day's pass bring you?

BEAVER   Nanabush, a pleasure as always. Toss me a twig by the edge, will you?

NANABUSH   Amik, what do you say to a game of stone toss? Or how about a race?

BEAVER   Sorry Nanabush, you know I am very busy this time of the season. Perhaps if you help me for the rest of the day, then I can spare a little time to play with you.

NANABUSH   Ha ha ha! You can't trick me into working today. If you think building a dam is so much fun, then you just go ahead and build your own damn dam. Today I am going to have fun.

In the distance we hear the sound of DUCKS.

CHORUS   Listen Nanabush! What is that sound? Are they friends of yours? The sound is too tempting to resist for you, isn't it? Listen to it. Listen to it. Follow it.

NANABUSH follows the sound of the DUCKS—offstage.

SQUIRREL   Acorns… seeds…. A nut or two? Where can they be? The acorns, seeds, or the one or two nuts? *(stumbling across RED and PINK rosebushes)* Oh! Pardon me…

CHORUS   What did you find, little one? Beauty? Sweet fragrances blanket the area. Patches of deep reds and soft pinks as far as the eye can see. Beauty and a sweet fragrance possessed by gentle ones. It is this gentleness they share that will prove to be their vulnerability.

PINK   Grandfather Sun, we give our thanks for your warm, comfortable blanket.

RED   Father Sky, we give thanks for your precious rains and clouds that allow us to whisper, dance, and sing with our brother Noodin. Dear sister, why won't our brother Birch give thanks?

PINK   He is much too proud. Having the strongest bark in the forest he feels invincible.

RED   Poor Birch. Will you change your cold ways? Nothing good could possibly come from them.

PINK   Will you open your heart?

BIRCH   No!

SQUIRREL   Birch where can I go for a nut or two?

BIRCH   Don't bother with me. No one else does. They know better. Leave!

SQUIRREL   I'm sorry. I am. *(to ROSEBUSHES)* You are beautiful, you are. Where would one like me find the seeds and acorns your brothers and sisters leave?

RED   Try the edge of dear Nanabush's garden. You will find plenty.

PINK   You will also find seeds, acorns, and maybe a nut or two by the garden of rocks, little one.

SQUIRREL   I thank you, gentle-petalled ones. I thank you.

CHORUS   Scamper off, find the treats you crave, and leave your thanks with all you take. Will Squirrel find more than seeds and acorns? After all, this is a tale or is it two, of Nanabush the trickster? Oh Squirrel, what predicament will follow? Listen: the forest is alive with sound, movement, and emotion. Listen who goes there? A Rabbit, a Raccoon and a Bear?

> *Enter RABBIT, RACCOON, and BEAR. SQUIRREL runs to greet them.*

SQUIRREL   Hello all. I'm looking for seeds and acorns, and a nut or two, I am.

RACCOON   Well keep looking; we're busy ourselves.

RABBIT   *(to BEAR)* I'm hungry. How about you?

BEAR   Yes, I'm hungry.

RACCOON   What should we eat today?

RABBIT   Let's try something different. I get tired of eating grass and clover all the time.

RACCOON   But we've tasted just about everything.

RABBIT   No. Not everything. We've never tried Nanabush's rosebushes.

RACCOON   That's right!

BEAR   Nanabush's rosebushes? I wonder if they will taste good?

RABBIT   There is only one way to find out. Let's go find them.

BEAR   I don't know if that is such a good idea. Nanabush can get really angry. I remember this one time he—

RABBIT   Nanabush won't find out. Besides, are you not the most hungry of us?

BEAR   Yes but...

RACCOON   Don't worry. We won't get caught. I am the most crafty.

RABBIT   I have the fastest legs to outrun any danger, and you're the strongest, so you have nothing to worry about.

BEAR   Don't the both of you tire of getting into trouble? I will not have anything to do with your plot.

RABBIT   Then it's your loss. Let's go, Raccoon.

RACCOON   Imagine, the biggest forest-dweller is also the most cowardly, HA HA HA!

SQUIRREL   What should we do, Bear? We can't let them harm those beautiful-petalled ones.

BEAR   We will call for Nanabush; he will know what to do.

CHORUS   You naughty creatures, scampering to the defenceless ones to ease your own appetites. They saw patches of red and pink as far as the horizon, pondering, what to consume first. Petals? Leaves? Nibbling, eating, and gobbling Pink and Red's sisters into their fat insatiable tummies. Eating like this takes work, and with work comes sleepiness. Grandfather Sun's rays beckon the two for a nap. The two friends could not resist.

PINK   Oh dear sister, there are only a few of us left. I'm afraid we too will soon be discovered and eaten.

RED   What can we do? All we can do is wait for our inevitable future.

PINK   But Nanabush loves us flowers. Why don't we send for help?

RED   Let us do this then.

CHORUS   Look, Red sister. Look, Pink sister. It is your brother, Noodin. He could not help but hear your cries. He invites you to ride on his backside. He knows the lands, the forests, the moves, and loves of Nanabush the wise. Let us follow and see what will prevail...

> *NOODIN and ROSES exit. DUCKS enter with a dance, throwing their eyeballs high into the air. NANABUSH follows.*

NANABUSH   Greetings my friends. What are those round shiny things you are tossing in the air?

DUCKS   Our eyeballs.

NANABUSH   That looks like a lot of fun. May I play your game with you?

DUCK #1   We're sorry, but you cannot play this game with us.

NANABUSH   Why not?

DUCK #1   Because you never listen when we tell you the rules to our games.

DUCK #2   And then you cannot "obey" the rules because you never listened in the first place.

DUCK #3   And worst of all, you don't always keep your promises!

ALL DUCKS   We just can't trust you!

CHORUS   Oh Nanabush, what will you do? Will you use your cunning? Maybe your strength will help you. Tell us Nanabush, will your cunning ways get you what you want? Maybe you have to do what's most difficult.

NANABUSH   Please, friend Ducks, may I play this game with you?

DUCKS   No!

NANABUSH   Please!

DUCKS   No!

NANABUSH   Please!

DUCKS   No!

NANABUSH   Pleeeeeeeaaaasssse!

DUCKS/NANABUSH   Ah fine then!

NANABUSH   What? Okay let's play.

DUCK #1   But you have to stop when we tell you to stop.

NANABUSH   Yah, yah yah.

DUCK #1   Promise?

NANABUSH   Yah, yah, yah.

DUCK #2   Nanabush, do you *promise*?

NANABUSH   Yah, yah, yah, I promise, now let's play.

> *The DUCKS and NANABUSH begin to dance and throw their eyeballs higher and higher with each throw.*

DUCK   Stop! Don't throw your eyeballs up anymore. The time has come to end the game.

NANABUSH   Awwww. Don't be so frightened, my billed friends.

CHORUS   *(gasp)* Nanabush! You promised. You promised! Will there be a lesson to be learned? What do you all believe?

NANABUSH   Just once more! Higher than ever before!

DUCKS   Nanabush! No don't, please.

CHORUS   Up and up and up, shiny round eyes in the sky looking down on Mother Earth, wondering how a view like this was possible. Oh silly Nanabush, what have you done unto yourself this time? Eyeless, with friends on their way to seek guidance. Whatever will you do?

NANABUSH   I'm blind! I'm blind!

> *NANABUSH, looking for his eyeballs, runs into BEAR and SQUIRREL.*

BEAR   Nanabush, what is wrong? Why won't you look at us?

SQUIRREL   Nanabush, we need your help, but it looks like you need help yourself!

NANABUSH   Please friends, leave me be. I do not know what to do for I can no longer see.

CHORUS   Poor Nanabush, your cries are being followed by your brother Noodin. What will your brother think of you? He listens, as do the gentle-petalled ones, then they recount the tale of the insatiable appetites of the greedy ones. Oh Nanabush, is this time to be one with blinded eyes? Perhaps if all the dwellers of this land stand and work as one, you will all change this tale's outcome…

> *They all help NANABUSH back to the garden.*

PINK   Follow our sweet-scented trail, Nanabush.

RED   Let our fragrance guide you to your beautiful garden. Maybe someone here will help you.

> *NANABUSH, trying to find his way around with blind eyes, runs into BIRCH.*

NANABUSH   Brother Birch, is that you? Look to me and help me. Please. I cannot see!

BIRCH   You have been given all of my brother's gifts, and all of my sister's beauty. Why not ask them for help? I cannot be bothered with your nonsense. In fact it serves you right! Did you not listen to the rules of their silly game?

RED   Brother Birch, how can you remain as cold as winter's grip?

PINK   Leave him, Red. He will never change.

> *NANABUSH, still trying to find his way around, runs into SPRUCE.*

NANABUSH   Who is this?

SPRUCE   It is I, Spruce. Take some of my gum, shape it as you like, and you will find it will work to your delight.

NANABUSH takes the gum and fashions eyeballs out of it and places them in his eye sockets.

NANABUSH   I can see! Thank you! Thank you, my friend Spruce. *(goes to see RED and PINK)* I will now help you. I am going to give you many small, needle-like thorns to cover your branches and stems. These thorns will not spoil your great beauty, but they will make anyone who tries to eat you wish they hadn't.

RABBIT and RACCOON enter. All the friends hide and wait to see what will happen. They go to eat the ROSES and soon enough we see them in intense pain from eating the thorns.

CHORUS   Devious and greedy ones. Mouth like a porcupine's backside. You fall, Rabbit. You run, Raccoon. How silly for you two. This was not what you planned for. But it is what was to be.

NANABUSH   Thank you, my friends, for bringing me home, and for watching over each other.

PINK   Thank you, Nanabush, for your precious gifts.

NANABUSH goes and gathers some willow branches and heads straight for BIRCH.

RED   Nanabush, what are you doing with sister Willow's branches?

NANABUSH   So you will not help others? Perhaps these marks will remind you of your callous ways. Your bark will no longer be sparkling, white and strong. It will peel and you will help my people by providing it as a gift to them.

We see a stylized whipping of BIRCH with the willow branches.

CHORUS   Lessons shared and learned. Nanabush? What adventure will you and your friends embark on next? Can we follow? Can we recount? Do you have a choice?

Nanabush and the Chipmunk

A council of animals seems to have been called together. BEAR seems to be heading it up. Any combination of animals could be present.

CHORUS   Do you hear the flustered voices like we do? Where are they coming from? Why now? What could it mean? Let us go see. Perhaps a friend or two may be there.

BEAR   We all must come together and plan some way to stop man from killing so many of us! A council of war has been called. We, the four-legged ones, the winged ones, and the finned ones must fight back! Man is becoming selfish!

RABBIT   Selfish!

FOX   Greedy!

WEASEL   Greedy!

BEAR   Killing many more of us than is necessary for food and clothing!

ANIMALS   Selfish and greedy!

FOX   But what can we do to stop him? Man has such powerful bows, arrows, war clubs, and he is very smart.

BEAR   Man is smart and his weapons are powerful, but in numbers, there are more of us. If we work together we can combine our gifts to outsmart man.

ANIMALS   Outsmart man!

BEAR   We can outrun man!

ANIMALS   Outrun man!

BEAR   We can out-strengthen him!

ANIMALS   Out-strengthen him!

BEAR   And we can prevail!

ANIMALS   Outsmart, outrun, out-strengthen man!

INSECT   Perhaps we can win this war against man. That is, if we do most of the fighting for you.

All the animals laugh at the little insects.

RABBIT   How could weak little insects like you help us?

INSECT   We can spread sickness and disease to him. Don't laugh too soon. Give us a chance, and we shall show you just how powerful we insects can be in our own way.

FOX   What have we got to lose?

RABBIT   Let's give the insects a chance. Perhaps they are strong in their own way.

FOX   Perhaps they can save us.

BEAR   Then you shall go, insects. Go with all our blessings and prevail against the two-legged ones.

ANIMALS   Prevail!

CHORUS   And away the tiny ones went. Flying. Looking for the wigwams where man slept, ate, and lived. Many days, many nights, relentless torment, the stings, dirtiness, and for some, the last aspect of man's cycle met.

MAN   What is making us so sick?

WOMAN   Why are the mosquitoes and flies so much worse this year?

MAN   I have not enjoyed a peaceful night's sleep in so long.

WOMAN   And I fear my last-born will not make it through the season's pass.

CHORUS   Panic spreading among the two-legged ones, war waged, hope leaving. The four-legged ones, the winged ones, and the finned ones rejoiced and celebrated the work of their little brothers. Their spirits soon turned to alarm. Nanabush the spirit was returning home from a long journey. They also noticed he was not alone. Chipmunk was with him.

WOMAN   Nanabush! You've come home.

MAN   Help us…

NANABUSH   What is happening?

MAN   We don't really know. Many of us have become sick!

WOMAN   And a lot of us have died…

MAN   If you don't help us soon, none of us will be left.

NANABUSH   Have you noticed anything different in the time I have been away?

WOMAN   The insects are very bad this year. Perhaps they are making us sick!?

NANABUSH   Chipmunk!? I want you to find out why my people are sick and dying. Find out if this truly is the work of the insects.

CHIPMUNK   Yes, Nanabush. I will find out what is happening to your people.

CHORUS   Make way, little one. Hurry! Hurry!

The animals have again gathered in the council circle when CHIPMUNK enters.

BEAR   Chipmunk, what brings you to our council?

CHIPMUNK   Your council of what?

BEAR   Our council of war!

CHIPMUNK   Are you responsible for the sickness and death of Nanabush's people?

BEAR   We asked our brothers the insects if they would help us destroy the two-legged ones. Man has become selfish!

ANIMALS   Selfish!

BEAR   Greedy!

ANIMALS   Greedy!

BEAR   And killing many more of us than is necessary for food and clothing.

ANIMALS   Selfish and greedy!

CHIPMUNK   Is it your place to decide the fate of the two-legged ones?

BEAR   Why should they decide our fate?

CHIPMUNK   Because that is the Creator's way. We all have a purpose in this circle we call life.

BEAR   You sound like one of them.

CHIPMUNK   All I'm saying is…

BEAR   Enough! If you do not fight with us, then you fight against us. You and your family will no longer be recognized as a four-legged one.

> *BEAR lets out a ferocious growl and CHIPMUNK runs off as fast as he can.*

CHORUS   No longer a four-legged one! And he ran. Ran as fast as his legs could take him. Find Nanabush and recount the tale that was passed on to you.

> *He finds NANABUSH.*

NANABUSH   Friend Chipmunk, why are my people sick and dying?

CHIPMUNK   I cannot lie to you, Nanabush. The animals have joined the insects in a war against man, because they feel man is destroying too many of us.

NANABUSH   You have chosen to tell me this? Won't the animals see you as a traitor?

CHIPMUNK   I feel this war has gone on long enough. I've always liked man, and if man has learned his lesson, I can give you the secret that will save your people from the insects.

NANABUSH   Please tell me anything you know that will save my people.

CHIPMUNK   Wait here.

> *CHIPMUNK runs off and brings back medicine to NANABUSH that will heal his people from the insects.*

CHORUS   Scamper, search…. You know how to treat such injustices, but beware, the tiny ones are not happy with your ways. They see all and like to recount. They notice that man is regaining strength and speed. What will they do? There is one who will not enjoy what will now be.

INSECT   What will we do?

RABBIT   We must kill Chipmunk for being so friendly with man.

FOX   I will surely make a meal of him!

BEAR   And I will use his measly bones for toothpicks. Let us find him and teach him a lesson he will never forget.

ANIMALS   A lesson he will never forget!

BEAR   It will not take us long to find the Chipmunk. I know he will be outside of man's village, watching and helping him. We will sneak up on him and then… pounce! I will grab him by the back of the neck and I will not let go. Let us punish the one known as the traitor!

> *We see the animals do as they say and pounce on CHIPMUNK. As they are mauling him, black stripes down CHIPMUNK's back should appear where there were none before.*

CHORUS   Our dear little friend. What will become of you? For doing what was right, why are you to share in what is so wrong? Chipmunk will you escape this torment that has been inflicted upon you? Perhaps Nanabush will bestow upon you good fortune. Maybe a lesson will be passed and passed. Maybe someone will not only hear this story, but listen to it as well.

NANABUSH   My friend Chipmunk, because you cared enough about my people, even though we were not always good, and because you saved them, everyone will know your story. From now on all your children, your children's children, and their children will also bear marks on their backs. This will remind man of his once greedy and selfish ways. This will also remind man of your loyalty to him.

CHORUS   Go, Chipmunk. Scamper and share your story with all; remind those who stray from their path with the tale of your backside. Live as you will, Chipmunk, for you will share many more tales, and we shall see what is forthcoming.

Mandamin

CHORUS She can no longer weave a basket. Sometimes when Noodin speaks, her ears do not listen. When Biidaasige-kwe waves hello, she appears to ignore her. She now knows she must prepare for a journey that only belongs to her. A part of this journey includes the sharing of a dream.

NOKOMIS I am growing old, my grandson. I will be leaving you for a while.

NANABUSH What do you speak of, Nokomis?

NOKOMIS I have been preparing for a journey I must take.

NANABUSH Where are you going, Nokomis? Can I come?

NOKOMIS My dear grandson, you cannot come with me this time. There are still many things you must do here. That is why I asked you to visit me before I leave.

NANABUSH Can you tell me a story? Tell me the one of the man who went fishing with the crow.

NOKOMIS No, Nanabush. I have to tell you something you must do for our people, something wonderful.

NANABUSH What will I do that will be so wonderful, Nokomis?

NOKOMIS I had a dream last night. I dreamt of a great battle between a warrior on the other side of the lake and you, Nanabush.

NANABUSH You must tell me more, Nokomis! Did I defeat him?

NOKOMIS The warrior was fierce and endured much pain, bearing a powerful stick, and Mother Earth shook every time the warrior stepped. Nanabush, you must cross the lake, defeat this warrior, and many rewards will be bestowed upon our people. This reward will be wonderful.

NANABUSH What will this warrior look like? What if I can't defeat him? What if I bring only shame to our people? Nokomis, what if—

NOKOMIS Just do what I have told you, my grandson. Look inside for the strength you will need, and remember all the things I have taught you and you will be able to defeat anyone. Now I must finish preparing for my journey just as you must prepare for yours.

NANABUSH Why must I defeat this warrior, Nokomis? What does this have to do with your journey?

NOKOMIS You must go now! Hurry. When you come home you will see what this all means.

CHORUS   Nanabush the great! Nanabush the wise! What will you need? What do you have? You will embrace many sunrises, and many sunsets on the dancing waters. Are you prepared? Are you going to bring your people the rewards your Nokomis speaks of? Or will your fears bring you failure. Tell us, Nanabush the great, the wise, what will you bring?

NANABUSH   I will bring rewards!

CHORUS   Nanabush! The lake awaits. Travel this day, brave one; time does not wait, the rewards must be fought for.

> *NANABUSH is becoming annoyed by the CHORUS voice.*

NANABUSH   *(to the voice)* Would you mind?! I need to pack.

CHORUS   Our apologies.

> *NANABUSH continues to pack for his journey.*

He prepares, he ponders. Nanabush, don't forget the dream. Don't forget your Nokomis's wise words. Hold on to them like a mother to her newborn life. Nanabush, look inside for the strength you will need.

> *We change our focus to SEAGULL and FISH. SEAGULL is trying to entice FISH to the surface.*

SEAGULL   I bet you cannot even jump as high as a grasshopper.

FISH   I can too. I only choose not to.

SEAGULL   What? What? Come a little bit higher and say that again. I did not hear for Noodin is also talking to me up here.

FISH   I am not easily fooled. Brother Lake is also talking to me down here and he says to stay low and beware the sneaky winged ones.

SEAGULL   What? What? Come a little higher and say that again. Grandfather Sun wants to tell us something.

FISH   I will not fall for your tricks, Gaiashk. I prefer the caress of Brother Lake's finger than chance one of your lies.

SEAGULL   What? What? Come a little higher and—wait…. What is that? Brother Lake brings a stranger with him. It's Nanabush!

FISH   I will not fall for it! Fall for it I won't! What would mighty Nanabush be—

NANABUSH   Doing here? I am travelling to the other side of the lake in search of a mighty warrior.

FISH   Nanabush!

NANABUSH   Aanii, brother Gaiashk, sister Giigonh.

SEAGULL   Tell us of this warrior you are searching for?

NANABUSH   He is fierce, he carries the mightiest of sticks, and he is so strong that Mother Earth trembles when he is around. Do you know of this warrior?

FISH   Perhaps you are looking for Mandamin.

NANABUSH   Who is this Mandamin you speak of?

SEAGULL   Mandamin is the fiercest warrior of his clan. He stands taller than any two-legged one, he is dressed in the shiniest of yellow and green garments, and on his head he wears a roach of nodding green plumes.

FISH   I've heard stories of many mighty two-legged ones who have tried to defeat him, but not one was successful. Why must you defeat Mandamin?

NANABUSH   My Nokomis told me of a dream that I am to defeat this warrior Mandamin, and if I use all that I have learned, my people and I will be rewarded with wonderful things.

FISH   Then you must go! According to the stories, Mandamin lives to the west of the shore.

SEAGULL   Be brave and strong, Nanabush.

NANABUSH   I will, my friends.

NANABUSH leaves and SEAGULL and FISH continue where they left off.

SEAGULL   I bet you cannot skip along the top of the water, like the smallest of flat rocks.

FISH   I can too. I only choose not to.

SEAGULL   What? What? Come a little higher and say that again, I didn't quite hear you…

The two move off stage as NANABUSH hits the shore.

CHORUS   Nanabush. What do you think now? Will you still face this mighty mysterious one? Many have tried and none have succeeded. What will you do that will be different from the others? Mighty sticks, a trembling Mother Earth? Nanabush, be brave! Be strong!

PORCUPINE, TURTLE, and DEER enter.

PORCUPINE   I heard that Woodpecker deserved it!

TURTLE   Really? I heard he lost control and that Woodpecker was in the wrong place at the wrong time.

DEER   You're both wrong. Woodpecker did it to himself.

   PORCUPINE and TURTLE both gasp in shock.

NANABUSH   Hello, my friends.

TURTLE   Nanabush, it has been too long.

DEER   What brings you to these parts?

NANABUSH   I have been sent by my dear Nokomis. She tells me of a dream where I am to defeat the fiercest of warriors.

DEER   You must speak of the one they call Mandamin.

PORCUPINE   Nanabush, are you aware that he has never been defeated?

NANABUSH   I am aware. Nokomis tells me how it is possible to defeat him. She tells me to use all that she has taught me.

   The three laugh at him.

DEER   He is a giant!

TURTLE   He carries a warrior's stick larger than you!

PORCUPINE   All tremble in his path!

TURTLE   You will need more than words.

PORCUPINE   More than words!

DEER   You will need all the help you can get.

NANABUSH   But Nokomis told me of the way it must be.

PORCUPINE   Did Nokomis ever face the mighty Mandamin?

TURTLE   Has Nokomis ever ventured into the village of Mandamin?

DEER   We all share this land with him; we know more of Mandamin than anyone.

TURTLE   Perhaps you may want some help.

NANABUSH   Maybe you are right. Perhaps Nokomis may be wrong, but who will I get to help me in this battle?

TURTLE   Maybe I can help. You will need a shield to protect you from the thunderous blows of Mandamin.

PORCUPINE   And what warrior goes to battle without a weapon? I can provide as a quill-covered club.

DEER   I will be your swiftness. Ride me as you would a steed on the plains I have heard about, and you will be the mightiest opponent Mandamin has ever faced.

NANABUSH   Let us go my friends, and let us defeat the warrior Mandamin!

ALL   Defeat Mandamin!

> *The four set out to find MANDAMIN.*

CHORUS   Silly Nanabush! Foolish Nanabush! To close your ears and heart to the one that loves you, who teaches you! Silly Nanabush! This was not to be the way of it. Foolish Nanabush, to have to learn this way. The Directions shake their head in disbelief. This is to be your journey, but very well, follow these three to the west and face what will be.

TURTLE   This is the village of Mandamin.

DEER   What shall we do?

NANABUSH   We will wait for him to appear.

PORCUPINE   Perhaps we will not wait too long.

> *The earth shakes and MANDAMIN appears.*

MANDAMIN   I am the one they call Mandamin! The great Creator has revealed to me in a dream that I am to battle the one he calls Nanabush!

NANABUSH   I am the one called Nanabush. I have been told by Nokomis I am to face you in combat and bring back wondrous rewards to my people.

MANDAMIN   It will not be easy. Many have tried, but none were successful. Should you defeat me, you will bring back the rewards to your people. Do you still wish to face me?

NANABUSH   Yes!

CHORUS   Nanabush be strong! Nanabush be brave! Look inside yourself!

> *NANABUSH, TURTLE, PORCUPINE, and DEER charge MANDAMIN. A choreographed fight scene takes place with MANDAMIN triumphing.*

MANDAMIN   This is enough for today, Nanabush. Return tomorrow and heed your Nokomis's words.

CHORUS   What will you do different tomorrow, Nanabush? Will you seek more help? Will you leave, head bowed in shame? Tell us, Nanabush? Your own way wasn't enough, was it? Now that a new day is upon us, what will you do differently?

> *The four face off against MANDAMIN again in a choreographed fight scene.*

You use a shield, Nanabush, but was this to be the way?

TURTLE gets injured, cracking his shell.

Was a quill-covered club ever spoken to you in Nokomis's dream, Nanabush?

PORCUPINE gets injured losing many, many quills.

And what of a steed's speed? Were our backs turned and missed this part of your dear Nokomis's dream, Nanabush?

DEER gets injured and limps away.

MANDAMIN   We will fight for the last time when we embrace the morning sun, Nanabush.

DEER   I will call my sister; she is just as fast as I, Nanabush. Maybe then we can defeat him.

TURTLE   And I will seek my uncle, he is—

NANABUSH   No! I will face Mandamin alone.

NANABUSH sits quietly as though in meditation awaiting the morning. We hear the rumble of MANDAMIN and the third and final battle takes place with NANABUSH prevailing.

CHORUS   Another day is upon us Nanabush; will you heed your Nokomis's words? This will be the final battle; look inside for your courage! Look inside for your strength! Use what Nokomis has taught you. The warrior is weakened with truth. Defeat him! He is weakened with your obedience! Throw him! Strip him of his garments! This is the way of it! Travel to whence you came and bury the warrior's remains there.

NANABUSH takes MANDAMIN's garments back across the lake and buries them when he returns home. NOKOMIS enters.

NANABUSH   Nokomis?

NOKOMIS   I am here, Nanabush.

NANABUSH   I found the warrior you spoke of…

NOKOMIS   And?

NANABUSH   I defeated him, but Nokomis? I am confused; what did all this have to do with this journey you will embark on?

NOKOMIS   I want to make sure you will be strong, and that you will be able to take care of yourself, because I will be gone for quite some time, and I won't be here for much longer to protect and teach you. Do you understand what I am saying to you?

NANABUSH   Yes, Nokomis. I understand.

A stalk of corn grows where MANDAMIN's garments once lay.

CHORUS   Time passed; once a grave now bears life, tall, beautiful, and proud. The Creator would see many feasts and thanks for the gift that was bestowed on all, and Nanabush shared the tales of the warrior with many generations as he would with this one…

Nanabush and the Spirit of Thunder

The sound of rain fades in; flashes of lightning and the rumbling of thunder begin to accompany the rain until it is the sound of a complete storm.

Enter the THUNDER BEINGS. They run around the stage, creating a kind of chaos. The sound of the storm begins to meld into a beat to which the THUNDER BEINGS begin a synchronized dance. The THUNDER BEINGS exit at the end of this music piece. A moment of silence and the storm comes back in at full force again.

Enter RABBIT and three or four other animals. They are very frightened by the loud thunder. Trying to find shelter, they bump into one another, running back and forth, echoing the earlier chaos at the beginning of this scene.

Enter NANABUSH—the sound of the storm remains. NANABUSH examines the situation, seeing the animals in chaos. He tries to stop the animals, but not one will listen. Finally he grabs hold of RABBIT by his now long ears.

NANABUSH   Rabbit! Why are all the animals afraid again, huh?

RABBIT   The great Spirit of Thunder is unhappy with us and is making so much noise. We are all frightened.

NANABUSH   Is this because of you again!?

RABBIT   No, Nanabush. I haven't done anything wrong this time. I haven't. I promise. Go ask any animal.

NANABUSH   All right then. Go, Rabbit.

RABBIT   Thank you, Nanabush.

RABBIT exits and the THUNDER BEINGS enter, creating chaos again. Sound still accompanying.

CHORUS   Why does this Thunder and Lightning and Rain pour so hard and heavy. Nanabush, you must find and send your bravest warrior to see the Spirit of Thunder. He must go to Thunder's home.

Addressing the audience.

NANABUSH   Which one of you will make the journey to see Thunder to find out why he is unhappy with the people of the forest?

CHORUS   The crops are being drenched and no one dares to see the angry Thunder. It is you, Nanabush. You must go, brave one, wise one, strong one.

NANABUSH   All right. If it is to be me who should go and see this great Thunder, then I will go.

> *NOODIN (wind) and fellow WIND SPIRITS come and carry NANABUSH as close as they can to THUNDER's home*

CHORUS   And he travelled much further than this, for he swam through the great floods of Thunder's skies. The sounds of great Thunder roared. The closer Nanabush came, the more fearful he became. But Nanabush the brave one approached the great Thunder. Now see what happens next…

> *We see the great THUNDER creating his storm. NANABUSH approaches him.*

NANABUSH   I have come here to see you, great Thunder.

> *THUNDER does not notice, nor hear NANABUSH.*

(*louder*) I have come here to see you, great Thunder!

THUNDER   Ah! Nanabush, sorry I did not see you.

NANABUSH   The people, the animals, fear that you are unhappy with them and that is why you make such dark and treacherous storms. Thunder, do you hear this? The animals fear that they have done something terrible and that is why you punish them with such long days and days and nights and nights of thunder and lightning. They are growing scared of you, Thunder. I have come to see if this is true. What have they done to make you so angry?

THUNDER   I am not angry with these animals. It is not their fault that it has been dark and cold. I have been creating this rain and thunder and lightning because I grow angry with the Sun.

NANABUSH   The Sun? I have not seen the Sun in weeks. I have only seen the darkness and the clouds.

THUNDER   The Sun had been shining many, many days. And for so many moons, I have not had to time to replenish the earth. The ground had grown dry, and devastation would surely come to the people. And so I create this thunder and lightning. I do not speak with the Sun!

NANABUSH   You do not speak to the Sun?

THUNDER I will not speak with the Sun! I leave it up to you, Nanabush. I have told my story.

NANABUSH Then I will speak to Sun for you. I will go seek him now.

> *NANABUSH begins to make his way to SUN's home and it grows warmer and warmer.*

CHORUS In this immortal world many things happen, and many things "can" happen. Nanabush had been taken to the place where the Sun lives. He rides a cloud of Thunder. This world is immortal and, remember, this is also Nanabush's home. But in this sun it grows warm, and Nanabush grows weary and tired. He tries to stay awake...

> *Enter SUN.*

NANABUSH I have travelled from very far, and I am growing tired.

SUN Nanabush! It is you! I've seen you coming this way from such a long distance. You have come to see me? Yes?

NANABUSH I am so tired, Sun, I cannot stay awake. It is so warm here; it makes you just want to lie down and rest.

> *NANABUSH lies down and falls asleep.*

SUN Sleep if you must, Nanabush. But you did come here to see me and not to sleep. Nanabush? Nanabush?

CHORUS He sleeps in a beautiful slumber. The Sun has made it so warm one almost cannot stay awake. But we are here for a reason. We will wake him. Nanabush! Nanabush! NANABUSH!

NANABUSH What?

CHORUS Nanabush, the story, you must finish the story and talk to the Sun about Thunder.

NANABUSH Thunder? Yes! Thunder. Dear Sun I am here to inform you that our dear friend Thunder has been very angry with you for many days and many nights as you have refused to stop shining and now Thunder has refused to let it stop thunderstorming. This has created many problems for the people and animals of the forest. They have become fearful of his great powers.

SUN Dear Nanabush, what can I say? I have been shining, yes. And shining, yes, and shining, yes! But I have also been extremely tired, and have been known to sleep in this beautiful warm weather as well. I am afraid I have fallen asleep. Now I am not sure how many days this has been. It was never my intention to anger anybody. Nanabush, you must go and tell Thunder what we shall do...

CHORUS   And the Sun and the Thunder created a co-existence in the sky world that lasts to this day. From that point, it would rain whenever the crops needed rain, and the Sun would shine whenever the crops needed sun. And Nanabush travelled back to the village, and the balance was once again restored.

Nanabush Punishes the Raccoon

CHORUS   Nanabush, the young brave soul, we see you! The great one, he had built a great relationship with his elders, his advisors, his people of council; they have endured the consequences of many hardships, hard times of war, disease, and devastation. Through this many good times have come out of this great cycle. For now we see these advisors who have become blind. For the many years of war, hunting, and gathering, their eyes have also grown with them.

Enter two old blind men, REGIS and ISSIE.

ISSIE   You said you'd never been down that trail, and now you say you know it like you were travelling it daily. How can that be? If you've never been down that trail, then how is it that you know it? What can you tell me that I don't already know?

REGIS   I never said that! You listen to my words for a change. Always getting lost in translation. I told you, I knew the trail years and years ago, but now it has changed. What is it that you can't keep up a conversation with me?

ISSIE   Ah! You're always changing your mind, that's what it is. Don't do this. *(drops his walking stick)* Do this instead! No change here. Where's my stick? *(He begins searching the ground for his stick.)* I just had it a second ago. Do you have it?

REGIS   I'm just as blind as you. I think that's it right there by your foot... your other foot!

ISSIE   I don't know how you can go on any trail, when you can't even— oh! Oh there. Here it is. I got it.

REGIS   See I told you!

ISSIE   I can't see very well, that's all. Always got something to say about everything.

Enter NANABUSH.

REGIS   Don't forget that we have that smoked meat on the fire, eh? It should be done now. Come my friend, let's go eat.

NANABUSH   Hello Issie, hello Regis.

REGIS   Ah! Hello Nanabush.

ISSIE   Good day! Good day, Nanabush. It's good you've come. We're going to have some meat and tea. Care to join us? I think I made iron wood. No. Wait. It's… oh yes, yes I think it's iron wood. Would you like some? Come. Come.

NANABUSH   Actually, my great uncles, I have come to put that line up you had asked for. I brought some of this rope. I thought it would be a good idea to do it today.

ISSIE   I don't need that old rope.

REGIS   Issie, you're the one always having a hard time; just let him put it up. It's not going to get in the way of anything. It's just a little bit of help, that's all. No big deal.

ISSIE   Regis, I don't need help. I'm fine. I'm going to get that tea. Are you coming?

>   *ISSIE heads off in the wrong direction.*

NANABUSH   Ahhh… this way, Issie. (*redirecting him in the right direction*)

ISSIE   Right, right, I knew that.

NANABUSH   I'll just put the line here, okay Issie? And if you use it, then use it. And if you don't need it, well then, don't use it.

ISSIE   Nanabush, you just do whatever then. I probably won't need it, but this old guy next to me might. Regis has a hard time finding his wigwam. Maybe you should tie the rope from him, to his wigwam, ha ha ha!

>   *NANABUSH ties one end of the rope to the men's house and the other end of the rope close to the river. The rope is intended for the men to follow to make it easier to fetch water.*

CHORUS   And so, he ties a line from the water to their homes, just like they had asked, this Nanabush. What a caring soul! What a brave mind! The generous Nanabush.

>   *NANABUSH completes his task and exits where the two men exited.*

NANABUSH   (*as he exits*) Okay, dear uncles, it is done. I also brought you some more smoked meat. Next time I'll have some of that great smoked salmon you both love so much.

>   *As NANABUSH exits, RACCOON and RABBIT enter from the opposite side of the stage.*

RABBIT   Why don't you try? You'd love it and it's so delicious.

RACCOON   No. Sorry. I will not do that.

RABBIT   Why? All you have to do for me is sneak in quietly. Look around yourself, slowly grab a piece of the petal, and then you grab the whole bushel and run! Nanabush will never know; besides he would never think it's you. He knows you don't eat petals; I know you don't eat petals.

RACCOON   So?

RABBIT   So it doesn't matter if you get caught. You won't get in a whole lot of trouble.

RACCOON   No, I said I wouldn't do it and I mean it. Now would you mind just leaving me alone?

> *RABBIT trips over the rope that NANABUSH has tied.*

RABBIT   Hey what's this?

RACCOON   Looks like a rope to me.

RABBIT   Where do you think it leads?

RACCOON   Don't know. Don't care. Come on, there's some fish up this way. I had some yesterday.

RABBIT   Okay, but wait!

RACCOON   Nope. I'm not going to wait this time. I waited for you last time and I ended up waiting for three days! Three days! I still don't get why you took so long at a molehill. A molehill. A molehill!

RABBIT   Moles have good food, and nice dens.

RACCOON   Yep. See ya!

> *RACCOON exits and RABBIT follows a bit behind.*

RABBIT   Okay, I'm coming; don't wait. I don't really want to know where that rope leads to. No, there might even be food at the end of it. You think?

> *Enter REGIS and ISSIE.*

REGIS   Oh, I'm sorry. I didn't mean for you to drop the whole pot of tea. I was just passing you the salt.

ISSIE   Well I can't do twenty things at once. I'm not that much of a… *(searching for the rope)* Hey where's that rope? Didn't Nanabush say he put a rope here?

REGIS   Right here, Issie. I got it right here, man. I thought you said you didn't need that old rope?

ISSIE   Ah, just hand it to me!

REGIS   Okay, okay. *(hands ISSIE the rope)*

ISSIE   *(taking the rope)* Hey it's not too bad. Easier, isn't it, Regis?

REGIS   Yep, Nanabush. He's a good man that one.

ISSIE   Okay, I think I know where I am now. Here's the water.

REGIS   Here, I have both the pots. Here, take this one.

> *ISSIE takes the pot and fills it with water.*

ISSIE   Hey, did you remember to cover that meat?

REGIS   Oh I forgot all about it! Hurry up; last time some animal ate our meat, remember that?

ISSIE   I know, I know. Let's go. Hurry. But don't spill it.

CHORUS   Hurry, dear men. Hurry back, so that you will not have lost your dinner. This rope is a handy rope. It will bring you home sooner than without. Hurry men. But who is watching? Someone peers from a distance. A curious one. What do they want? Why do they wander around here?

> *RACCOON enters again and begins examining the rope.*

Raccoon? What are you doing? You are looking rather suspicious, little one.

RACCOON   Where does this rope lead to? Rabbit said… actually Rabbit didn't say. Let's see, if I follow it to where those two old men went… it goes to their home, and if I follow it this way, it goes to the… water. I get it! I get it!

> *RACCOON thinks for a brief moment.*

Oh! I think I am going to have some fun…

CHORUS   Raccoon, you were always such a good one. What are you doing? Do not trick these old ones; they may help you someday.

> *RACCOON takes the end of the rope that was at the water and places it at the opposite end of the stage, and waits for the old men to go get more water.*

They will not need water for at least another day, Raccoon. You waste your precious time. Go find something useful to do.

> *Enter ISSIE with the rope thinking he is making his way to the water.*

ISSIE   I knew he would spill it. Now I have to boil this water all over
again. Why can't that old guy just do something right for a change?
Why... he's always trying to do this and that... make things more
difficult, make it even harder. Even when we used to hunt together,
taking the long route.... Those deer don't take the long route, I would
tell him. Why do you think they use that trail? It's their trail, I would tell
him, and no. *(reaching the end of the rope)* He always had to go out and
find himself in the wrong place and then I would find him in the... hey?
Where is the water? This is the end of the rope. But where is the water?
Oh dear! The river has dried up! What on earth shall I do? Go back and
tell Regis. He'll know what happened. He'll know. Regis! Regis! The
river! Regis!

> *Continues to call for REGIS and exits off stage. RACCOON lifts
> himself up from behind the bushes laughing uncontrollably and
> carries the rope back to the water and hides in the bushes again.
> ISSIE and REGIS enter again, as fast as they can go, which is not
> very fast.*

REGIS   What do you mean it's dry? We were just there. It can't dry up that
fast. That's impossible.

ISSIE   You'll see for yourself. Just wait till we get to the end of the rope.
We're almost there.

> *They reach the end of the rope and ISSIE reaches down to find water
> again.*

What on earth is happening here? Here is the water again!

REGIS   I may be as blind as you, but I'm not a fool! You tricked me!

ISSIE   I never tricked you, and how do you know it was I? Maybe it was
you who did this...

REGIS   Maybe you just wanted me to carry that water back home
because... because.... "My arms are tired and sore, Regis. You carry
this," eh? How do I know for sure?

ISSIE   It's not all because of that Regis.... So what if you carry it back.
Somebody did something; there was no water here, none at all.
I wouldn't have come back to get you if it weren't true. I don't know.
Something is not right...

> *RACCOON, still laughing, goes to the rope and follows it back
> towards the wigwam then exits the stage and re-enters with the
> men's meat, eating and laughing. REGIS and ISSIE begin to make
> their way back up to their home.*

REGIS   Not right. I will tell you this is not right. I come all the way down here 'cause you said there was no water, and now there is? What am I supposed to think, eh?

ISSIE   Your supposed to listen. I don't know what happened Regis, but we'll just go back home and pretend this never happened, okay? Here you go first—

REGIS   The river dried up! How can a river dry up in a day? Rivers take seasons to dry up; didn't your father teach you anything?

ISSIE   Okay, enough, the river is there. It's still there. I'm sorry.

REGIS   What did you say?

ISSIE   I said the river is there.

REGIS   No, that last part. What did you say?

ISSIE   It's still there!

REGIS   No, no, no…

ISSIE   Oh all right, I'm sorry, okay. I'm sorry I made you come all the way down to the water, I'm sorry you had to get up. I'm sorry, I'm sorry, I'm sorry.

REGIS   Nahowdush!

ISSIE   Let's go eat!

> *They follow the rope off stage and notice their meat is gone.*

REGIS   *(from offstage)* I'm tired of your tricks today! *(entering)* Why did you take my two pieces of meat?

ISSIE   I didn't take your meat. You are just trying to make trouble today!

REGIS   Oh, I'm not the one who's making all the trouble today. You are making trouble. Why isn't my food there? It's supposed to be there!

ISSIE   I don't know where you put your food.

REGIS   It was in that pot and you, you took it. I know you did. That's why you wanted me to go down to that river, so you could eat my food, that's why.

ISSIE   That is not the reason. I have my own food and I can eat it myself. I don't need to eat yours. Yours is undercooked anyway.

REGIS   It's not undercooked.

> *RACCOON who has been watching all this laughs hysterically from behind the bush. He runs up between the two men and hits both of them in the stomach at the same time.*

ISSIE   Oh! Now you want to hit me. Is that it?

REGIS   You hit me first. Let's go, old guy!

ISSIE   We'll see who the old guy is.

> *They begin to fight and roll around on the ground. NANABUSH enters and sees the old men fighting. RACCOON has been laughing so hard he doesn't notice NANABUSH enter. NANABUSH grabs hold of RACCOON.*

NANABUSH   What have you been up to, Raccoon?

RACCOON   Just visiting. I must leave now.

> *RACCOON tries to escape but NANABUSH won't let him.*

NANABUSH   Oh no you don't!

ISSIE   Nanabush, is that you? I followed that rope down to the river but it had dried up and then it was there again.

REGIS   And then someone took our meat, Nanabush. I think someone planned this on us.

NANABUSH   *(to RACCOON)* So you like to play tricks on old blind people? I think I'll show you a trick or two.

CHORUS   As punishment, Raccoon endured the humiliation and pain of Nanabush placing eight black charcoal rings on his tail, representing the meat he had stolen, four rings for each piece of meat. And because he was mean to those old blind men, he made his eyes bad. He will never stand the sunlight again. Poor Raccoon, forced now to hunt at night forever, and the task of washing all your food before you eat it. All this to remind you of the terrible trick you played. Go Raccoon. Go.

> *RACCOON exits, head bowed in shame. NANABUSH helps REGIS and ISSIE off stage.*

Nanabush and the Spirit of Winter

> *The sound of cold, harsh winter wind fades in. Small drifts of white appear.*

CHORUS   This winter, it is harsh and it is possible for an entire village to freeze to their deaths. You must remember, in these times winters can be a time of devastation, death, and tragedy.

REGIS   Nanabush, what has happened to my village? This is not right. This cold air, this snow. This layer of freezing temperatures, what will become of my village if this cold continues?

ISSIE   One must go north. One must talk to that North. You should go, Regis.

REGIS   I can't do that anymore. You're the younger one. You should go, Issie.

NANABUSH   Gentlemen, I will go. I've been to that North before, and although I have only heard of this Winter Spirit, I will find him and I will speak with him. I must get ready for my long journey.

> *ISSIE and REGIS exit and NANABUSH begins gathering things for his long journey.*
>
> *Music fades in, NANABUSH makes his travel, and more and more billowing cloths of snow appear and cover the entire stage. NANABUSH sees a huge creature covered from head to toe in frost and icicles. Cold, icy winds pour out of his nose and mouth.*

I must not let him know I am afraid. Okay. Who are you?

WINTER   I am the Spirit of Winter. Who are you to invade my land?

NANABUSH   I am Nanabush… the spirit. I have much to say to you.

WINTER   Nanabush… the spirit? You mean Nanabush the trickster, do you not?

NANABUSH   Why yes, some do know me as Nanabush the trickster. You are much smarter than I thought. I guess I will never be able to play any tricks on you…. Winter? Why do you make this land so cold? Why do you not sleep once in a while and let the land warm up?

WINTER   That is really none of your business. Why should the land not be cold?

NANABUSH   Because of all the Indian men, women, and children. You are making life hard for them.

WINTER   Ha ha ha! I make cold weather, dear Nanabush. That is what I do. And cold is what it is.

NANABUSH   I am… oh great Winter, in need of rest. Do you have any food here?

WINTER   I eat snow and ice. If you would like some, then please help yourself.

NANABUSH   No thank you. Ice and snow probably taste really good, but I prefer rice, meat, and herbs.

WINTER   What is this rice, meat, and herbs? Are they good?

NANABUSH   Why yes, they are very good, but I doubt you would like them.

CHORUS   At that moment Nanabush started a small fire and put on a pot of rice, meat, and herbs to cook. Soon the food filled the air with a beautiful aroma.

> *NANABUSH begins to eat, overly enjoying the food.*

WINTER   This smells delicious, Nanabush. May I have a taste?

NANABUSH   I don't think you would like this, Winter, and besides it's not quite ready.

WINTER   When it is ready, might I try some?

NANABUSH   Well I don't know…

WINTER   Please, Nanabush. It smells so good.

CHORUS   Well, as you can guess, the very persistent Winter would not let up until he had a taste of the wonderfully aromatic dish. And of course, Nanabush would be the one to give him that taste.

WINTER   This *is* delicious! May I have some more? I am enjoying this hot food.

NANABUSH   Eat all you want, my friend. I can get more for myself later on.

CHORUS   And the Spirit of Winter ate and ate and ate this delicious, hot bowl of traditional foods. And from eating so much, he began to melt, suddenly realizing Nanabush's trick. But poor Winter could not stop eating, for it was so delicious. And soon the cold winds stopped, the sun became warm, and the snow and ice began to melt everywhere.

> *WINTER begins to melt and melt as does the snow-covered stage.*

WINTER   *(melting off stage)* I'll be back, Nanabush! I'll be back!!!

Nanabush and the Dancing Ducks

CHORUS   Nanabush. Where does the strong and brave wise one come from? Where did he go? For this Nanabush has been on many levels of wisdom, a dignified man, a respected Nanabush. Some days he is just off, and clumsy, and strange, for this day is not his day. Nanabush? We see you; what are you thinking?

> *NANABUSH enters gathering bits of wood. He stops when onstage.*

NANABUSH   I'm hungry. Actually, I'm starving!

> *He continues to gather bits of wood and begins to pile them for a fire.*

Oh what a sweet piece of dried meat would taste like right now.

CHORUS   What is this sound we hear? A rumble? Is this the great thunder again? Is this the buffalo galloping this way? What approaches this place?

NANABUSH   Actually it's me. I really am starving. You wouldn't happen to have any food would you? Some fish, deer, dried cranberries? Anything?

CHORUS   Nanabush, we are afraid we have no food to offer you. How sorry are we. Can we offer you anything else?

NANABUSH   No. I should just build this fire.

> *NANABUSH builds a fire centre stage. While he is building the fire the sound of DUCKS can be heard from off stage.*

CHORUS   Nanabush! Wait! We hear a sound in the distance. It summons you. They sound as if they were horns in the sky. They are birds, Nanabush. Ducks, Nanabush! Have you called for ducks?

NANABUSH   No, I haven't. But ducks would be great right now. Duck! And not just one, oh no no no no. All of them. Yes, all of them. I could just eat every single one of those beautiful, flying birds.

CHORUS   Be careful, dear Nanabush, for we sense something wrong about this.

NANABUSH   Nonsense. I know what I'm doing. Can you just leave me be now, please. I'm busy. I know! I must call them; I must prepare my best duck call *(pause and deep breath)* Yoo hoo! Friends! Ducks! Come and see. I feel we have not connected in a long while. You must come and play this wonderful game with me. It's brand new. I've just created it today. I am also very excited that you beautiful Ducks will be the first ones to learn to play this game. I'm sure it will become so popular and such a hit. Perhaps even a new trend! Who knows?

> *DUCK #1 (CLIVE) and DUCK #2 (RUFUS) come in for a landing. RUFUS, however, makes a crash landing. DUCKS #3 and #4 come in shortly after.*

CLIVE   Oh we do love your games, Nanabush. We are, however, behind schedule because Rufus here set us back two days!

RUFUS   It wasn't my fault. Look, the wind was blowing from the north; I've told you this already. And you are completely aware that going against the north wind is one of my biggest challenges. I told you, remember? I said, "Clive, this north wind is getting stronger; maybe you should take the lead." Remember? But you said, you said, "No Rufus, you're doing a fine job. It's all good. You have nothing to worry about."

Remember that? Huh? Everybody was there. You guys remember, don't you?

> *Looking to DUCKS #3 and #4 for support but they are not paying any attention to what is going on.*

DUCK #3   Oh man, I think I need some water.

DUCK #4   Water? Wait! I'll come with you. Just a sec, I need to fix my cramped wing. (*He releases his tension and becomes loosened.*) Okay. There we go. Let's go get that water.

> *They make their way to the side of the stage where there is a jug of water waiting for them.*

RUFUS   Well, are we going to play or not!

CLIVE   With an attitude like that I don't think you should be allowed to play.

RUFUS   All I did was ask a question.

CLIVE   I think someone is getting angry.

RUFUS   (*tensed, trying not to let out the anger*) I'm not getting angry! I'm not getting angry. Breath! Breath. Deep breaths…. One, two, three, four, five, six, seven, eight, nine, ten. (*deep breath*) Okay! I'm okay now.

CLIVE   (*to NANABUSH*) Rufus here is taking anger management.

NANABUSH (*amused by this all*) Don't worry, Clive. He can play, and besides, this game wouldn't be the same without all of you in it.

CLIVE   If he wants to play, it's up to him.

RUFUS   Yes! Yes, I'll play! Of course I'll play.

> *The other two DUCKS return.*

NANABUSH   Okay, here are the rules.

DUCK #3   Wait, wait, wait. What are we doing?

NANABUSH   I'm explaining the rules.

DUCK #4   Rules? To what? What rules? Do we have new flying rules? Is there a new migratory pattern? I never heard anything about any new migratory patterns, or new rules to them. Have you, Rufus? Clive?

NANABUSH   No, no, no. Rules to the game.

DUCK #4   (*shocked*) Whose game? Are we game now? It's not even hunting season, is it? Clive, tell him we're not game!

DUCK #3   I'm not going back up there if we're game now. Forget it! That's what happened to my cousin, flying so happy and then all of a sudden, foomp! Down, down, down to the ground. Dead! All because he was game!

DUCK #4 (*to CLIVE*) And I'm not going if he's not going. Uh uh, ahh, no way!

NANABUSH   No, wait stop please. (*He speaks very slowly and articulates every syllable as if to make everyone understand.*) WE ARE PLAYING A GAME… nobody here is game, well, not in this game… sorta…

DUCKS   What? Forget it! No way, I'm not playing any game where I'm game…

NANABUSH   Well, you're all game. I mean, admit it. You are game, right? That's what most people refer to you as, game. It's just game. But *we* are *playing* a game, okay, and you are not game, in this game.

> *Brief pause as everyone tries to make sense of what was just said.*

DUCKS   Oh? All right, okay… I'll play.

DUCK #3   And yes, we are in fact game!

DUCK #4   Wild game!

DUCKS   Yeah! Wild game, we are wild and we are game. Wild game! (*They stop and look at each other, realizing their destinies and what they are in fact celebrating.*) Ummm? Okay. Let's play!

NANABUSH   Yes, let's!

> *NANABUSH motions for them to come closer to him. He huddles them in a circle to explain the rules.*

CHORUS   Nanabush, he is still the trickster, tricking those whose trust is there. Nanabush, do not hurt these poor ducks with another trick.

> *NANABUSH and the DUCKS are still in the huddle as though NANABUSH has been explaining the rules to the game.*

NANABUSH   And remember the most important rule of them all—you *must* keep your eyes closed at all times.

DUCKS   Oh! I don't know about this.

NANABUSH   Come on, I promise it will be fun.

DUCKS   Okay, well since you promise.

> *NANABUSH begins to beat on a drum and sing a traditional song. The DUCKS close their eyes and begin to dance around the fire. As he is singing, he kills the DUCKS one at a time using various fun*

methods. After all the ducks have been killed, he places them all in the fire to cook with only their feet sticking out. NANABUSH, now tired from all the activity, begins to yawn, decides to take a nap, preparing a little bed for himself.

NANABUSH   Oh I am getting so sleepy. Who can watch these delicious ducks for me while I sleep? Hmmm?

Looks around but cannot find anybody, then turns to his buttocks and gets a wonderful idea.

I know! Behind. You will watch these ducks. I am so sleepy. The ducks will cook and when I wake, it will all be ready. Behind, do you hear me?

NANABUSH decides that his behind has heard him and lies with his buttocks high in the air toward the fire.

CHORUS   Nanabush, the trickster, he returns once and every so often performs some trick and only does harm unto himself. For look who has returned? It is the great Noodin, the mighty powerful Wind. Watch the Wind. What is it that he does?

NOODIN dances around NANABUSH and the DUCKS and decides NANABUSH must be taught a lesson for being so greedy. He takes all the DUCKS away leaving only their legs sticking out of the fire. NOODIN then dances offstage, waking NANABUSH with a slap to the buttocks as he exits.

NANABUSH   *(stretching)* What a great little nap. *(looks around)* Oh! Now I will eat the succulent delicious ducks.

NANABUSH waltzes over to the fire and pulls out a leg, and is surprised that it is only a leg.

What? I can't believe this!

Checks every leg and sees that they are all the same, only legs.

What is going on here? Who is playing a trick on me? Who? I demand you to come out now! Rabbit!? Raccoon?! Chipmunk?! Anybody!? *(to his buttocks)* Ah! Behind! This is all your doing! I know it was. I am so angry and disappointed with you, I will burn you on this fire, I will. Stand still!

NANABUSH straddles the fire.

CHORUS   And our brave and wise trickster, he burns his own behind touching it to the fire. The heat makes him scream, and shout, and cry. It is not all lost, Nanabush. Why, you did learn a lesson, did you not? Nanabush?

NANABUSH   *(running off stage)* YES!!!!

CHORUS   Our dear sweet Nanabush, never forget the lesson of the Dancing Ducks.

Nanabush and the Wild Geese

CHORUS   Green carpets Mother Earth and visits horizons on a beautiful afternoon. The river dances with the breeze, brothers, sisters, fathers, mothers, all acknowledging all that is good with Grandfather Sun. Where is Nanabush? Is he in trouble? On his own? Wait, new sound interrupts the breeze's conversation with the grassy ones, a snore. Nanabush... the sleeping? A little one is having his fun.

> *CHIPMUNK comes racing in.*

CHIPMUNK   Father Sky is landing for a visit! Father Sky is landing for a visit!

> *NANABUSH turns but does not awake.*

CHORUS   Nanabush embraces sleep and slumber. Will this get his attention?

CHIPMUNK   Father Sky is coming for a visit. Nanabush, look! Father Sky is coming for a visit.

CHORUS   The trickster is finally awakened to this excitable one. He also has no choice but to embrace hunger.

NANABUSH   Why the chatter? I had wonderful dreams of giant feasts in my honour after a day of brave deeds.

CHIPMUNK   Is that all you think of? Food? Here have some of my acorns—

> *CHIPMUNK throws some acorns at NANABUSH.*

CHORUS   Not a good idea, little one. Nanabush can tease and teach but does not always like to receive. Calm yourself, Nanabush; all this is in light spirit.

NANABUSH   I'm sorry; I just want something good to eat, like a big fat flock of geese.

CHIPMUNK   I have rope; here look, woven of the strongest corn silk. Now all you need is a flock tied to it.

NANABUSH   Hmmmm?

CHIPMUNK   All you need to do is go to the water bank, dive in, wait for the landing, tie them up, and eat them.

NANABUSH   Then that is what I shall do!

CHORUS Oh Nanabush, what will become of this ill-thought-out scheme? If only such plans were that simple. But if they were, perhaps we would not be here now. Oh foolish Nanabush, don't you know better? You will certainly reap what you are about to sow. Waiting in the water, embracing chills, then you see them plump and juicy and in hand's grasp. You are tempted to pounce, but you hold back? What is this change of plans?

NANABUSH You geese must be tired. Come and rest here at Mother Lake, and I will quench your thirst.

CHORUS Mother Lake?!

ELDER GOOSE Okay Nanabush, we have had a long trip.

Once all the geese have landed in the lake NANABUSH begins to tie all of the geese legs together with the rope

CHORUS Silly Nanabush! You cannot mix ill-thought plans with many years of wisdom. They know what is happening. They have flown for many days and tire of regular patterns. Do you not see, Nanabush, you are merely entertaining them?

GOOSE What do we do? He is trying to capture all of us.

ELDER GOOSE On my signal we shall show this trickster his own medicine. *(pause)* Now!

CHORUS What a sight! Wild geese flying everywhere, with the elder of the flock in the middle creating the shape of an arrowhead, all tied together. What will become of you, Nanabush? Falling faster and closer to your mother, the earth. Your little friend is also watching the excitement.

NANABUSH hits the ground hard, right beside CHIPMUNK.

CHIPMUNK Where's my rope?

NANABUSH simply points upwards.

CHORUS And to this day all the geese will fly in that formation. Will there be other tales of winged ones? Let's listen to the sounds and follow them where they may lead us.

The end.

The Indian Affairs

A few summers ago while in workshop development, the creation team for *The Indian Affairs* was sitting around outside under a tree working. The discussion led to the question of whether or not it was realistic that the dog—Maa-iin-gahns—was still alive in Act III, since twenty years had passed since it first appeared on stage in Act I. The conversation kept going around—amazing pet longevity stories, maintaining the high level of realism in the rest of the play, etc.

As it was necessary to make a decision about Maa-iin-gahns or no Maa-iin-gahns in Act III, the conversation turned serious. We all really loved the dog and thought maybe it should die during Act III, so at least we would all have a chance to say goodbye and pay our respects.

Finally, one of our guests from the city—a playwright—broke out in laughter. She pointed out that we were all so concerned about the believability of the dog's lifespan, but none of us had a problem with the fact that the dog talks to people and to wolves.

We were reminded once again that we were creating from a slightly different view of the world.

De-ba-jeh-mu-jig staff photo. Left to right: Elijah Kavanaugh, Shelagh Hughes, Elisha Sidlar, Tammy Manitowabi-Shawanda, Joseph Osawabine, Cotnee Kaboni, and Josh Peltier.

The Indian Affairs was created collectively by the company based on cultural teachings by the Odawa Midewin Lodge.

The Indian Affairs was first produced in 2005 by De-ba-jeh-mu-jig Theatre Group, with the following creation team:

Ron Berti
Shelagh Hughes
Elijah Kavanaugh
Cotnee Kaboni
Tammy Manitowabi-Shawanda
Joe Osawabine
Doreen Peltier
Josh Peltier
Evelyn Roy
Elisha Sidlar

Director:	Joe Osawabine
Stage Management:	Lori Anderson
Set and Lighting:	Ron Berti
Costume Design:	Bill Shawanda
Sound Design:	Joe Osawabine

Characters

STARLEE—better known by her friends as STAR, is the central character. She comes from an alcoholic family and tries really hard not to fall into the patterns of alcoholism and neglect that her parents had set forth for her. She is best friends with RONNIE and is the girlfriend of JIMMY.

JIMMY GWECH—also comes from an alcoholic family, his parents are also physically abusive, and he has anger problems. He is seriously looking for his place in the world and always has the urge to run away from his life.

CHUCK—comes from a single-mother household; his mother is promiscuous and always has guys over. This deeply affects CHUCK more than he will ever know or admit to and he grows to be quite the womanizer.

MATT—has never known a real home. He grew up in foster care, moving from home to home for a majority of his life. This has ultimately caused some real identity problems for him, and he is always trying to fit the mould.

RONNIE—probably the least dysfunctional in the bunch, but maybe more dysfunctional in her lack of dysfunction. She grew up in a stable home with both parents and has never had any real problems, but because she is from the Rez she thinks she knows the hard life and is always quick to offer advice.

ANNE—the only one not from the reserve, meaning she is white. She comes to us from any major urban centre and has been visiting the Rez since she was a little girl. She has grown a strong friendship with the rest of the bunch and sees things from the outside looking in.

MAA-IIN-GAHNS—STAR's dog and the link to the spirit world.

ZHANGWESH—Spirit wolf—representative of the spirit world—the ancestors.

WASSEN—Spirit wolf—representative of the spirit world—the ancestors.

The Indian Affairs

ACT I

The Clubhouse

Summer 1985. An abandoned hunt camp belonging to STAR's grandfather, situated not far from the community. The hunt camp has been converted into the clubhouse. Downstage left, atop a bluff, is a wolves' den, the home of ZHANGWESH and WASSEN, the spirit wolves.

A chalkboard inside reads "THE GRILS CLUB—NO BOYS ALOWED EKSEPT MATT."

The sounds of wolves howling surround the audience.

CHUCK (9) and JIMMY (8) enter stage left howling (sounding nothing like wolves), drinking Coke, and acting drunk with a ghetto blaster playing. They come across the clubhouse and CHUCK goes inside while JIMMY keeps watch in case the girls return. CHUCK changes the sign to read THE BOYS CLUB—NO GIRLS ALLOWED EVER EXCEPT MATT—CHUCK AND JIMMY ROOL!!!

They run off whooping in victory, singing along to the ghetto blaster. MAA-IIN-GAHNS (puppy) enters looking for the sound and who woke her up

MAA-IIN-GAHNS   (*directed towards audience*) All right who woke me up? What's the big idea, eh? Who was it? Was it you? Or you? Oh, I know it was you. I've never seen such a guilty look. What's the big idea, eh? Waking me up with all that howling…. Howling pffft! You call that a howl? I'll show you a howl.

MAA-IIN-GAHNS mocks the earlier howl heard from CHUCK and JIMMY.

ZHANGWESH and WASSEN, the two spirit wolves, are awakened by MAA-IIN-GAHNS's howling and enter stage right from their den looking for this strange noise as well.

ZHANGWESH and WASSEN always speak in a traditional language.

ZHANGWESH   Oh, Maa-iin-gahns we should have known. Maa-iin-gahns, stop that howling.

MAA-IIN-GAHNS   No no no no it wasn't me it was this person here.

*MAA-IIN-GAHNS directs them towards the audience member
she had picked out earlier. CHUCK and JIMMY are heard again
howling from offstage, again redirecting their attention.*

ZHANGWESH   There it is again, over there!

WASSEN   What are they trying to say?

MAA-IIN-GAHNS   Ah don't even bother trying to figure it out. I gave up
long ago; they have all sorts of strange howls these days. *(mocks the howl
again)* Yeeeeeeeee-oooooooooo

ZHANGWESH/WASSEN   *(looking at each other)* Yeeeeeeooooooo? *(looking
back at MAA-IIN-GAHNS)*

MAA-IIN-GAHNS   Oh baby!

ZHANGWESH/WASSEN   *(again looking at each other)* Oh baby?

MAA-IIN-GAHNS   O sixty-nine!

ZHANGWESH/WASSEN   *(again looking at each other)* O sixty-nine?

MAA-IIN-GAHNS   And I could go on but neh! *(MAA-IIN-GAHNS goes
to leave.)*

ZHANGWESH   Hey Maa-iin-gahns, tell us, what else has been going on?
Is there anything else we should know about?

MAA-IIN-GAHNS   Well if you want to know what's going on then you'll
have to figure it out for yourselves. I did!

WASSEN   How we supposed to do that, eh?

MAA-IIN-GAHNS   Just watch them.

ZHANGWESH   Watch them? They're supposed to be watching us.
Haven't you heard the legend of the first dream?

MAA-IIN-GAHNS   Yah yah yah, I know the legend of the first dream:
"watch the wolves" blah, blah, blah.... How are they supposed to watch
you? It's not like you see wolves every day.... I'm the one here... yet
nobody's dreaming about dogs! We have just as much to teach them as
you do!

ZHANGWESH and WASSEN laugh.

ZHANGWESH   What could they possibly learn from a Rez dawg?

*ANNE (7) has lost her way from her parents' cottage and can also be
heard.*

ANNE   *(from offstage)* Mommy?

MAA-IIN-GAHNS I'll have you know that my great, great, great-grandfather on my mother's side was a wolf... no no no, wait I think it was my great uncle on my father's side... or was it? Ahhh never mind I can howl like the best of them. Listen to this... owwwwwwwwwwww!

ANNE enters from stage left.

ANNE Great! Now I'm lost and there's wolves after me.

WASSEN Hey? Who is this stranger?

MAA-IIN-GAHNS Oh... I don't know... she's new.... I haven't seen her before...

MAA-IIN-GAHNS runs over to sniff her and ANNE gets startled.

ANNE Hey you're not a wolf... you're a dog.

MAA-IIN-GAHNS Grrrrrrrrrrr... I'll have you know that my great, great, great... something, on somebody's side was a wolf so that makes me part wolf.... Grrrrrrrrr.

ANNE Ahhh... okay... ahhh... nice doggy... it's okay... I won't hurt you.... Here.... Do you like balls?

Taunts MAA-IIN-GAHNS with the ball.

MAA-IIN-GAHNS Hey a ball! Throw the ball! Throw the ball! Come on! I'll bring it back I promise, just throw the ball, come on throw the ball.

ANNE Here doggy ahhh.... Go fetch.

ANNE throws the ball over and behind the audience, and MAA-IIN-GAHNS excitedly chases after it.

MAA-IIN-GAHNS Sucker, it's my ball now... rowf.

MATT *(offstage)* Maa-iin-gahns! Give me the ball ahhh... stupid dog! Wuss! Go home!

MATT (7) enters from behind the audience dressed as a cowboy, carrying the ball. ANNE, unaware of MATT's presence, is now headed towards the clubhouse.

ANNE Hello? Is anybody home?

MATT I'm here!

ANNE turns to see MATT and is startled.

ANNE/MATT AHHHHHHHHHHHH!

They have a moment of staring each other down and assessing the situation. Finally feeling that it's probably safe, MATT holds out the ball.

MATT   Is this your ball?

ANNE   Ahhh… yah… *(takes the ball).*

>   *ANNE is still a little alarmed and is looking at MATT very perplexed and somewhat nervously.*

Ummm… are you an Indian?

MATT   *(laughing)* No… I'm a cowboy.

ANNE   *(relieved)* Oh good! Cuz my mom told me to look out for the Indians.

MATT   Why?

ANNE   I think she's afraid of them.

MATT   Why?

ANNE   I don't know?

MATT   Did she say anything about cowboys?

ANNE   No.

MATT   Cuz she should be afraid of cowboys!

>   *MATT pulls out his guns and mocks shooting her. ANNE instinctively becomes an Indian and runs away from MATT and the traditional game of Cowboys and Indians ensues with ANNE retaliating with her bow and arrow.*

ANNE   *(stereotypically)* Whoo whoo whoo whoo whoo!

>   *As ANNE is running from MATT she steps on a sharp thing and hurts her foot.*

MATT   *(actual concern)* Did I kill you?

ANNE   No, I stepped on a sharp thing.

MATT   I'm a doctor. I can make you better.

ANNE   I thought you were a cowboy?

MATT   *(taking off cowboy hat)* No, I'm a doctor now! Come on.

>   *MATT takes her towards the clubhouse.*

ANNE   Are you gonna have to cut it off?

MATT   No, I think we just need some Band-Aids.

>   *They enter the clubhouse.*

ANNE   Do you live here?

MATT   Ummm? *(thinking about where he lives)* No, this is just where we play.

ANNE   Well where do you live?

MATT   I used to live at my aunt's house, then I lived with the Turners in a city, then I moved in with my other brother in that house over there behind the church, but I don't play with them... oh no... that was before... first I lived... over... *(giving up)* Aah? What's your name?

ANNE   Anne with an "E," I live with my mom and dad.

MATT   My name's Matt... with an "M." See?

> *Points to the blackboard where his name is and notices that the blackboard has been changed by CHUCK and JIMMY.*

Hey? Ah man! Chuck and Jimmy have been here.

ANNE   Who's Chuck and Jimmy?

MATT   They're boys and they go to our school but they're in four.

ANNE   Are they fun to play with?

MATT   Jimmy's okay but Chuck is... well he's...

> *RONNIE and STARLEE are heard from offstage left. They are singing Madonna's "Like A Virgin."*

ANNE   Who's that?

MATT   My friends. They're meeting me here.

> *RONNIE (8) and STAR (8) enter stage left. MAA-IIN-GAHNS runs over to meet them as MATT and ANNE come outside.*

Hi guys.

ANNE   Whose dog is that?

RONNIE   It's mine.

STAR   Nah uh, it was your dog last week. *(to MATT)* Who's she? *(referring to ANNE)*

ANNE   I'm Anne. *(pause)* With an "E."

MATT   She's my new friend.

ANNE   What's its name? *(referring back to MAA-IIN-GAHNS)*

STAR   Well, I'm Star and this is Maa-iin-gahns.

> *ANNE doesn't understand the dog's name and STAR sees her confusion.*

(very slowly) Maa-iin-gahns

ANNE   Your what?

STAR   My what?

ANNE   Iin-gahns?

STAR   Huh?

ANNE   Hello Iin-gahns!

Everybody is now confused.

RONNIE   I'm Ronnie and this is our clubhouse.

MATT   Was our clubhouse. Jimmy and Chuck were here. Come see.

They all go inside and see that the sign is changed.

CHUCK and JIMMY return with cigarettes and matches and are trying to smoke by the side of the house.

STAR   So! I'm not afraid of them.

STAR changes the sign again this time to read THE GIRLS CLUB NO BOYS ALLOWED EXCEPT MATT. CHUCK AND JIMMY ARE STUPID SAYS STAR AND RONNIE!

RONNIE   Yah, Chuck and Jimmy are stupid anyways. Let's do our video now. I have to be home for dinner. Anne, you could take Matt's place?

STAR   Why do you get to tell us what to do?

RONNIE   Cuz I'm the best.

MATT and STAR look at each other in disgust.

MATT   Well then what do I get to do?

STAR   You could be the cameraman.

MATT   'K! I'm the cameraman.

ANNE   No, you could be the director.

MATT   'K, I'm the director.

RONNIE   No. I'm the director.

Everyone stops and looks at her.

Okay you could be the director then but I'm Madonna, 'k? You have to go stand over here where the director goes and tell us what our moves are, 'k and you go on this side and you go on this side, and then you tell us our moves, 'k? 'K now they go like this, One, two, three, turn. *(continue ad lib depending on the dance routine)*

> *They go through their routine singing "Like A Virgin" with RONNIE wearing the bridal veil. She eventually gets tangled up in it and gets frustrated. By this time CHUCK and JIMMY are peeking in the window watching the girls.*

How you supposed to dance with this stupid thing?!

MATT   I'll show you.

> *MATT puts the veil on with the bouquet of flowers and begins the routine. CHUCK and JIMMY, seeing this, come bursting into the house.*

CHUCK/JIMMY   *(laughing)* Matt's gay! Matt's a fag! Matt's a queer. *(ad lib)*

> *MATT takes off the veil and is near tears.*

MATT   No I'm not! Shuddup—I'm the director!

STAR   Leave him alone. He's the director.

JIMMY   Well then who's she?

CHUCK   No. What is she?

STAR   Shuddup! She's our friend and she's in our clubhouse.

JIMMY   No. This is our clubhouse now. See, NO GIRLS ALLOWED!

CHUCK   Except Matt.

JIMMY   'Cause he's gay

STAR   No, this is my grandpa's land.

JIMMY   Nah uh, my mom told me that nobody could own the land.

CHUCK   Yah and how can he own it if he's dead?

STAR   I wish you were dead.

ANNE   Don't say that.

CHUCK/JIMMY   Who are you?

MATT   She's our friend.

STAR   She's our backup dancer.

MATT/STAR   She's our backup dancer friend.

RONNIE   She's Anne.

EVERYBODY   *(except CHUCK and JIMMY)* With an "E."

> *Everybody pauses and looks at each other.*

CHUCK   She's.... She's pink.

Uncomfortable pause; everybody looks at ANNE.

STAR   *(realization)* She is pink.

Everybody continues to examine ANNE.

MATT   I like pink.

ANNE   It's just 'cause I'm hot. Hey, I have Freezies back at our camp. But I don't know how to get back.

MATT   I'll go with you.

ANNE   'K. What colours do you guys want?

CHUCK   I want pink.

ANNE and MATT leave to get Freezies; RONNIE, STAR, CHUCK and JIMMY remain at the clubhouse.

JIMMY   Well this is still a boy's club, no girls allowed, except Anne, only 'cause she has Freezies.

STAR   Nuh ah, it's a girl's club, no boys allowed except Matt.

CHUCK   Well we're not going anywhere.

RONNIE   And neither are we.

JIMMY and CHUCK go stage left inside the house, and STAR and RONNIE go to the opposite side (split focus scene). Meanwhile MAA-IIN-GAHNS is marking the territory of the house as her own.

JIMMY   Geez I don't want to hang out with stupid girls.

CHUCK   Well where else are we gonna go?

JIMMY   Ummm… we could just go to my house.

CHUCK   Why? So your dad could beat us both up?

JIMMY   *(obviously hurt by the remark)* Shut up.

STAR   I don't want them here, especially Jimmy. He's always pulling my hair.

RONNIE   But they have a ghetto blaster.

CHUCK   Plus we can get the girls to do stuff for us, and we can hide things here.

JIMMY   Like what?

CHUCK   Like this *(holds out the stolen ghetto blaster)* and our smokes.

They turn to face each other again.

RONNIE/CHUCK   Okay you can stay.

STAR   No, *you* can stay.

RONNIE   *If* and *only if* you leave your ghetto blaster.

CHUCK   *(looks at JIMMY and then at the girls)* Okay.

EVERYBODY   Deal.

> *ANNE and MATT return with the Freezies.*

MATT   Star! Star! There's something going on at your house!

STAR   Just mind your own business!

ANNE   *(with genuine concern)* Yah there was some guy with his shirt off out on the lawn yelling something about…

STAR   I said mind your own business!

JIMMY   *(to MATT)* Was it my uncle?

> *MATT nods in affirmation. Everybody is quiet and sits down on the deck to eat their Freezies. MAA-IIN-GAHNS comes and sits behind the group, watching them eating.*

STAR   *(to herself)* What can you do? What can you do?

MATT/ANNE   What can you do when you live in shoe?

ANNE   Jinx!

> *Hits MATT on the arm.*

MATT   Jinx!

> *Hits ANNE on the arm. Everyone continues to eat Freezies.*

ZHANGWESH   Oh now they're quiet.

MAA-IIN-GAHNS   The only time you can get them to be quiet is when you shove something in their mouth. *(to each person)* Can I have some? Can I huh? Please? Can I have some? Please? Can I? Huh? Please? PLEEEEAAASE?

WASSEN   Look at that poor dog begging for food. Will somebody please feed that dog?

> *STAR feeds MAA-IIN-GAHNS some of her Freezie.*

RONNIE   All right everybody listen up, we've decided Chuck and Jimmy are in the club!

MATT   And Anne.

RONNIE/STAR   And Anne.

RONNIE   But the ghetto blaster stays here.

CHUCK   And nobody else is allowed.

JIMMY   Yah! Especially no grown-ups.

RONNIE   And we have to clean up after everybody.

> *RONNIE gathers up Freezie wrappers.*

MATT   And there's no name-calling me... I mean you can't call me... there's just no name-calling.

ANNE   And no hurting each other?

STAR   And this has to be our special place, and we have to be friends forever, 'k? Promise?

CHUCK   Promise.

JIMMY   Promise.

RONNIE   Promise.

MATT   Promise.

ANNE   Promise.

MAA-IIN-GAHNS   Arf!

ANNE   'K, now we have to pinky swear.

STAR   Pinky swear?

ANNE   Yah that means you can never break it.

> *ANNE demonstrates a pinky swear with MATT, and then everyone pinky swears each other.*

MATT   'K pinky swear, Maa-iin-gahns.

EVERYONE   *(laughing)* Yah pinkie swear, Maa-iin-gahns.

> *They all crowd around MAA-IIN-GAHNS and pinky swear.*

ANNE   Ha ha we just pinky sweared a dog.

JIMMY   Can you pinky swear a dog?

RONNIE   Let's celebrate now, oh I know! Come on, Matt, help me.

> *They go inside to get the bridal veil and the flowers. MATT changes the board to say THE GIRLS CLUB ALLOWED CHUCK JIMMY STAR RONNIE MATT ANNE.*

CHUCK   *(to ANNE)* Thanks for the Freezies; you know you're all right. Hey? Where did you get the big ones?

ANNE   My mom keeps them in the fridge.

CHUCK   Trade you moms.

JIMMY   *(to CHUCK)* Trade you dads.

CHUCK   I don't have a dad.

JIMMY   I know.

STAR   You can't trade moms and dads! You get what you get.

CHUCK   Matt trades moms and dads.

ANNE   Huh?

JIMMY   Well you know Matt? He used to live by the church with one of his moms.

CHUCK   Yah and then he got a different mom but not his real mom and…

> *MATT and RONNIE come back outside.*

RONNIE   Let's play wedding!

JIMMY   I don't wanna play wedding! Let's play hide and seek or something!

CHUCK   Yah, let's play wedding and then you can marry Star. You like her anyways.

JIMMY   Shut up! *(to STAR)* No I don't!

RONNIE   Yah, Star and Jimmy could get married!

MATT   And you girls could be those—princesses they have.

ANNE/RONNIE   Bridesmaids.

STAR   I don't wanna marry him.

CHUCK   And I'll be the one who marries them!

RONNIE   'K Chuck, you be the priest and Anne and I will be the beautiful bridesmaids, and Matt, you could be the best man and Star and Jimmy will be bride and groom.

JIMMY   I don't wanna marry Star.

STAR   Yah I don't wanna marry Jimmy.

ANNE   Just play, then I'll go get some more Freezies after.

JIMMY   Geez… 'k then.

RONNIE   'K, sing the song, sing the song.

> *Everybody hums the wedding march as STAR and JIMMY walk down the aisle.*

CHUCK   Dearly beloved, we are gathered here today...

> *Looks around for support but nobody seems to know what comes next in the ceremony.*

JIMMY   See we don't even know how to play this stupid game.

RONNIE   'K, now just skip to the part where he says, "Do you take this..."

CHUCK   Yah yah yah yah I know. 'K do you, Jimmy, take this stinky ugly...

MATT   Hey no name-calling. Remember we promised.

CHUCK   Ahhh... 'k... do you, Jimmy, take this... GIRL... to be you're awfully wedded wife.

JIMMY   This is dumb... I don't wanna play...

ANNE   *(enticingly)* Freezies.

JIMMY   Ahhh... 'k den.

EVERYBODY   Ha ha ha hah Jimmy loves Star... *(etc.)*

CHUCK   And do you, Star, take this... Jimmy to be your awfully wedded husband?

> *STAR looks at everybody assessing the situation. She looks at JIMMY who is looking at her, anticipating her response.*

ANNE/RONNIE   Just say "I do..."

STAR   I guess I do.

EVERYBODY   Ha ha ha ha Star and Jimmy are married... *(etc.)*

RONNIE/ANNE   *(whispering to CHUCK)* Now you gotta tell them to kiss.

CHUCK   Oh yah! You gotta kiss the bride.

RONNIE   You HAVE to kiss the bride.

JIMMY   Ah geez... I don't wanna play anymore.

> *JIMMY goes to run away but CHUCK quickly stops him.*

RONNIE   You HAVE to, Jimmy!

> *JIMMY and STAR look at each other shy and scared, and excited all at the same time. Inch by inch they make their way closer to each other. As they get close enough STAR closes her eyes in anticipation*

and JIMMY puckers up, eyes closed, and very quickly pecks STAR on the cheek.

Everybody screams and yells and laughs, grabs handfuls of grass and begins to throw it at the newlyweds.

EVERYBODY   *(singing)* Star and Jimmy sitting in a tree, K-I-S-S-I-N-G, first comes love, then comes marriage, then comes Star with the baby carriage.

Throughout this chaos STAR puts the veil on MAA-IIN-GAHNS.

RONNIE runs back in to the clubhouse and changes THE GIRLS CLUB to THE CULTURE CLUB.

JIMMY   'K let's play Hide and Seek now!

CHUCK   'K you're it then.

JIMMY   Ah geez 'k den 1... 2... 3...

Everybody runs and hides offstage.

4... 5... 6... 7... 8... 9... 10. Ready or not, here I come!

Eighties music begins to play.

Interlude—1985–1995

The music fades into the following audio montage of music sound bites, TV show sound bites, and communication among the six characters—letters being read, phone calls, etc., chronologically over the decade that passes. These should be recorded and mixed into the musical montage.

Stage crew ritualistically, and with great respect for the space and the house, change the scene.

*Matt and Star

MATT   Star, I don't want to go that way.

STAR   Don't worry, Matt; I'll just punch their heads out if they bother you.

*Matt and Jimmy

MATT   Hey Jimmy, can you borrow me twenty bucks till next week?

JIMMY   Uhhh... yah I guess, Matt... but now you owe me forty.

MATT   Yah yah… I know, I'll pay you back. I promise.

*Ronnie and Star

STAR   Where were you last night, Ronnie? I thought you were just gonna stay home and study. I tried calling.

RONNIE   Oh geez, Star… I forgot… Chuck and I—

STAR   Chuck and you?

RONNIE   …Yah.

STAR   'K, 'k I'm coming over. This I gotta hear.

*Anne

ANNE   Dear Ronnie, school's out thank god… but I am gonna be up a week later this year, 'cause my mom's transferring me to an ALL girls' school so I can "apply" myself. Which means any chance I had with Sergio, remember that guy I was telling you about? is totally shot down the drain…. I'll tell you more about it when I arrive…. Love Anne.

*Star and Ronnie

RONNIE   And then?

STAR   We kissed.

RONNIE   Well it's about freaking time.

STAR   What do you mean by that?

RONNIE   Oh come on, Star; everybody knows that you and Jimmy are gonna hook up.

STAR   Really?

*Star

STAR   Hi you've reached 4769. If you're calling for Star leave a message. I'll get back to you when I can. Those of you who care know where I am. Beep.

ACT II

"Welcome Home Star"

> *Summer 1995. The clubhouse is now transformed into STAR's house. The old table that was once inside the house now sits downstage right. Two old car seats are now set up against the wall of the clubhouse and a new table and couch are inside the house. Anything else can be substituted inside the old clubhouse to make it look more like a home and to give the illusion that ten years have passed. MATT (who is already slightly intoxicated and only gets more and more intoxicated as the scene progresses), JIMMY, ANNE, and CHUCK are hiding in the house to surprise STAR with a housewarming. STAR enters, dragging a bundle of her personal effects, everything she owns: clothes, dolls, pictures, etc. ZHANGWESH, WASSEN, and MAA-IIN-GAHNS are watching from their place on the hill.*

ZHANGWESH   Maa-iin-gahns, don't just sit there. Go help her.

MAA-IIN-GAHNS   Why don't you go help?

WASSEN   You're the only one here, remember?

MAA-IIN-GAHNS   Well you're here…. Oh… yah… right, spirit wolves! All right I'll go… *(under her breath)* Stupid spirit wolves… I wish I was a spirit wolf, sitting around all day… "Maa-iin-gahns, go do this, Maa-iin-gahns, go do that." Stupid spirit wolves.

> *MAA-IIN-GAHNS goes to help STAR but only ends up in the way.*

STAR   Ahhh geez Maa-iin-gahns, go! You're always in the way! I get more use out of a rock. At least the rock will hold the door open.

> *MAA-IIN-GAHNS sits down and looks at STAR with puppy-dog eyes.*

MAA-IIN-GAHNS   All right all right I can take a hint. I know when I'm not wanted.

STAR   Awww I'm sorry Maa-iin-gahns. At least *you're* here.

> *STAR goes to pet MAA-IIN-GAHNS behind the ear.*

MAA-IIN-GAHNS   Oh yah… that's good baby… right there… oh yah.

STAR   I mean, when you say your gonna freakin' do something, you should do it, right Maa-iin-gahns?

MAA-IIN-GAHNS   Oh yah uh huh oh yah baby… no no no… just a little to the left oh yah…

STAR   What the hell kind of a world would we live in if everyone just went around saying that they were going to do something and then never did?

MAA-IIN-GAHNS   Right there, right there! It's just you and me baby... just you and me.

STAR   A promise is a promise, right Maa-iin-gahns? *(baby talk)* I promise you'll always be my widow puppy wuppy and I'll wove you forever... *(continues to pet MAA-IIN-GAHNS)*

> *STAR goes back to work dragging her bundle.*

MAA-IIN-GAHNS   Hey? Hey? Where you going? Ahhh yah... love me and leave me.... You're just like the rest of them.

> *STAR struggles intensely with her bundle and she is extremely frustrated and upset and is crying by this point.*

STAR   Where the hell is everyone when you need them!

> *JIMMY, RONNIE, ANNE, MATT, and CHUCK rise up in unison from the attic.*

RONNIE   'K shh shh.

JIMMY   *(whisper)* Ah shit, she sounds mad.

ANNE   She is mad.

CHUCK   Maybe this wasn't a good idea.

> *Everybody lowers back down in unison.*

STAR   Why can't anything ever just work out the way it's supposed to!?

> *Everybody rises back up in unison singing STAR's favourite song. JIMMY is on guitar.*

JIMMY   Happy housewarming, Star!

> *They lower a banner, which reads "Welcome Home Star." STAR is obviously touched and moves from tears of sadness to tears of joy.*

STAR   Ever stupid, you guys. Geez... I thought I was alone. *(embarrassed)*

> *JIMMY goes over to STAR and they embrace and kiss.*

MATT   We'd never leave you alone, or maybe we should leave these two lovebirds alone

STAR   Thanks guys. This means a lot to me.

MATT   Are we just going to stand around here? Or does anybody want to party?

ANNE   Looks like you already started.

RONNIE   Of course we're gonna party but first we do gifts. Jimmy is obviously last... all right Chuck?

CHUCK   Ahhh...

> *CHUCK, unprepared and with no gift, begins looking through his pockets; finds a tape of recorded music.*

Here ahhh... this is a... ahhh... umm... ah... tape I made for you.

JIMMY   That's the tape she made you for your birthday, dumb-ass!

CHUCK   I recorded over it.

ANNE   *(to STAR)* Isn't that the tape you made for Chuck?

STAR   Shh, it's Chuck. What do you expect?

> *ANNE pulls out a plant.*

ANNE   Here, Star. I figured it would add something, you know.

WASSEN   She's giving her a plant?

ANNE   It's an African violet. It represents the virtue of friendship.

JIMMY   Awww.

ZHANGWESH   Aa-fri-kan vie-let?

MAA-IIN-GAHNS   From Africa.

WASSEN   What's it used for?

ANNE   You can just put it on the table.

> *STAR hands the African violet to JIMMY who takes it and places it on the table downstage right. MAA-IIN-GAHNS follows JIMMY and the plant over to the table.*

MAA-IIN-GAHNS   You put it on the table.

ZHANGWESH   Do you eat it?

ANNE   I figured it would look nice, you know.

MAA-IIN-GAHNS   No! You don't eat it... you look at it!

> *MAA-IIN-GAHNS sits and stares at the plant on the table.*

STAR   Awww thanks, Anne.

WASSEN   Well then what?

MAA-IIN-GAHNS   You just look at it!

> *MAA-IIN-GAHNS continues to sit and stares at the plant.*
> *RONNIE and MATT go and get a quilt.*

RONNIE   'K close your eyes!

> *JIMMY stands behind STAR and covers her eyes while the other two*
> *prepare for the unveiling of the quilt.*

One, two, three, tadah!

STAR   Holy shit, Ronnie, this must have taken you hours.

RONNIE   Yah it did take some time. It woulda taken longer but Grandma
and Mom helped.

STAR   Thanks, Ronnie.

RONNIE   And we picked all your favourite colours. It's all natural fabrics
and I double lined it twelve stitches per inch and...

STAR   Thank you, Ronnie.

> *STAR admires the quilt.*

It really is beautiful.

MATT   'K my turn. I got you this rock.

ZHANGWESH   Ahhh... a gift that makes sense.

CHUCK   A rock?

MAA-IIN-GAHNS   I think it's to hold the door open.

MATT   It's not just any rock. I've had this rock since the first house I lived
in with my real mom and dad. This is your first house... I want you to
have it now.

ANNE/RONNIE   Awww.

RONNIE   That is really sweet you know when you think about it... all the
places that Matt has been. It's like his whole life has gone into it... kinda
like my quilt... when you really think about it...

CHUCK   It's a rock.

STAR   Thanks, Matt.

RONNIE   That's everyone? All right now gather round everybody for the
soulful sounds of Jimmy Gwech, as he's known around these parts.

JIMMY   Ronnie, can I see you inside for a sec?

> *JIMMY and RONNIE go inside the house and look out the window.*

RONNIE   Okay? What's up?

JIMMY   All right, here's the deal… I don't think I can sing in front of everybody.

RONNIE   Why?

JIMMY   I'm not drunk enough yet.

RONNIE   Okay…

> *Goes back outside.*

Okay everybody, let's go inside, give these lovebirds some privacy.

> *JIMMY and STAR move over to the firepit.*

JIMMY   I wrote a song but… it's not ready yet, Star.

> *Everybody else goes inside to give them their privacy, except CHUCK who listens at the window or door.*

ANNE   Chuck, get out of there. Just let them be. I mean, would you want somebody watching you when you were trying to have a private moment?

CHUCK   Ah, yah, actually.

ANNE   That's creepy…. Okay I'm curious, what's going on?

> *JIMMY can't find the right note and has several false starts. JIMMY finally starts his song.*

CHUCK   He's chickening out.

> *Everybody goes to get a vantage point on STAR and JIMMY.*

RONNIE   What? He better not be! I mean, do you know how many times I've had to listen to that song today.

CHUCK   Yah I've heard it once or twice myself.

MATT   He just needs a drink.

ANNE   'K be quiet you guys. He's going for it.

> *The following is an original song composed by Joe Osawabine (can be substituted).*

E   B
It's late Friday night and you're knocking on my door
A   E
I've been waiting on you and I'm ready for more
                                 B
I look into your eyes and see reflections of your soul
A   E
I saw a little piece of me in you and nobody knows

```
E                 B
```
I get so damn lost in your longing gaze
```
A                        E
```
You swept me off my feet in a thousand different ways
```
E      B    A          E
```
You take me away, so far so far away
```
E            B    A          E
```
And you take me away, so far so far away

> *At the end of the song WASSEN howls very softly and mournfully.*

STAR   Hey did you hear that?

JIMMY   Hear what?

STAR   Never mind, it was beautiful... I loved it, Jimmy...

> *They kiss.*

I... I love you. *(almost under her breath but sincere; this is the first time STAR has told JIMMY she loves him)*

> *JIMMY doesn't respond and looks a little stunned or caught off guard.*

I said, I love you.

> *CHUCK is flabbergasted and runs three quarters of the way across the house and realizes that he hasn't heard JIMMY's response and goes back to his place in a panic.*

JIMMY   Yah... I ahhh...

MATT   Oh my god is he gonna say it back?

ANNE   Shh shh!

JIMMY   I ah... Star, I... yah that's cool.

> *MATT and ANNE are flabbergasted and run three quarters of the way across the house doing their version of CHUCK's earlier thing and run back to the window.*

CHUCK   Yes buddy! The closest word to love is leave.

STAR   That's it? I finally work up enough to tell you I love and all you got is "that's cool"?

JIMMY   Ah come on, Star, you know I do.

STAR   Do what?

JIMMY   That I... you know... I...

RONNIE   Love her! *(tries to stop herself but can't help it and immediately covers up her mouth with her hands)*

JIMMY   *(turning to see everyone watching them)* Have you guys been listening this whole time? Why don't you guys mind your own freaking business!

> *JIMMY goes back to where STAR is and she is obviously pissed.*

Come on, Star, why do you gotta be like this?

STAR   Just go! I don't wanna see you right now! JUST GO!

> *CHUCK comes outside carrying various bottles of booze in an attempt to diffuse the situation.*

CHUCK   Ah come on Star... you know he loves you. We all love you... now let's party!

> *RONNIE, looking for a distraction, comes out of the house carrying the board game Life. ANNE pours herself a drink inside, drinks it down in one shot, and fills two more glasses. She heads outside as well, handing the second glass to RONNIE. MATT has two bottles, one of Southern Comfort and one of Johnny Walker.*

RONNIE   Who wants to play Life?

> *Enlisting MATT's support in the situation, she nudges him to come and play.*

MATT   *(sarcastic)* Yah okay let's *play* life; oh can I be red huh? Can I, can I?

RONNIE   Yes, you can be red, and I'll be blue.

> *JIMMY goes towards the table and CHUCK meets him halfway.*

CHUCK   *(mocking STAR)* I love you, Jimmy.

JIMMY   Shut up!

CHUCK   No 'k seriously... what you going to do? You can't tell her now!

JIMMY   I know... just get us some drinks.

> *JIMMY goes to hand STAR a bottle of Malibu, which she refuses.*

STAR   I don't want that! Just go, I said!

> *JIMMY leaves and stands with his back to STAR and drinks the entire bottle.*

RONNIE   Hey who else wants to play Life? I'm setting up the board... Chuck can be yellow, Jimmy could be orange... and Star you could be... *(looking to STAR)* pissed right off... *(Without anyone else seeing, STAR* *begins to gesture for RONNIE to come to the firepit.)* at some... body... oh... who could it be?...

> *RONNIE sees STAR gesturing but tries not to tip JIMMY off.*

MATT Could it be... Mr. Orange?

STAR Look, Ronnie, I don't want to play Life. *(STAR is still motioning for RONNIE to come to the firepit.)*

RONNIE Well I brought Risk too... it's a little longer... but... *(stands up)* or I know, I could run home and get Clue.

> *RONNIE makes her way past JIMMY who moves over to the other end of the stage to be alone for a minute and gather his thoughts.*

STAR Ronnie, you get a clue all right. Just here, let's make a fire so it's not so obvious 'k?

> *RONNIE goes to the firepit and she and STAR begin to build a fire. Meanwhile MATT has been playing Life all by himself, moving around the board to be each player. JIMMY sits in thought while CHUCK and ANNE, sitting on the step, continuously get flirtier and flirtier with each other.*
>
> *CHUCK and ANNE head down to the table.*

ANNE *(to CHUCK)* I don't want to play Life, do you? *(flirting)*

CHUCK *(oblivious to ANNE's flirting)* Nah man, not really.

> *CHUCK notices JIMMY alone.*

MATT *(to ANNE so that CHUCK doesn't notice him)* Then why don't you two go in the house and play doctor. *(gesturing towards the house)*

> *MATT goes back to the game quickly and abruptly as though nothing was just said as CHUCK turns around.*

So let's see, who goes first? *(spins the contraption)* And Matt goes first. *(takes a drink)*

ANNE *(to CHUCK)* Brrr... it's cold. *(flirting again)*

CHUCK *(oblivious again)* No, it's not.

ANNE Well I'm gonna go inside. The mosquitoes love me.... Are you coming?

CHUCK Well... let's go then.

> *They go inside.*

MATT And it looks like Chuck goes next.

CHUCK goes to enter the house and realizing how ungentleman-like it would be to enter before ANNE, he lets her enter first.

Oh no. Wait. Anne goes next.

ANNE is whispering in CHUCK's ear and he is obviously very excited by whatever it is she has just whispered to him.

CHUCK   No way! Really? 'K ahhh... just let me get a blanket.

ANNE continues upstairs and CHUCK comes out to talk to JIMMY quickly as he passes by MATT.

MATT   Oh my! That was quick.

JIMMY   Hey, Chuck.

CHUCK   Jimmy! Jimmy I'm gonna... you know we're gonna... you know Anne... *(motions towards the house)*

JIMMY   What? Chuck, what the hell are you doing man! Hello! That's Anne!

CHUCK   I swear I didn't even try this time.... It's just... it's just happening, you know how it is, man. *(with reverence)* It's Anne.

JIMMY   Well what about Ronnie, eh? What are you gonna tell her?

CHUCK   Oh yah! Shit! *(thinking)* Ah shit we just... fool around.... She knows that.

JIMMY   *(big sigh)* Whatever, man.... I got my own shit to figure out.

CHUCK   All right then! I'll be back.

CHUCK heads back inside and scoops up the quilt that RONNIE had made for STAR on his way in. MAA-IIN-GAHNS follows him but the door shuts in her face as she goes to enter. She then goes down to the fire pit with STAR and RONNIE. CHUCK goes upstairs to ANNE.

MATT   And Jimmy goes back to start and Matt takes a drink. Things are finally starting to heat up in the game of Life.

STAR and RONNIE are at the firepit by now.

RONNIE   So what's going on, eh? It really means a lot to me that you would pick me to talk to.... Not a lot of people confide in me for some reason.... 'K so what's going on... I'm all ears... you know I really think...

STAR   Ronnie, just shut up please!

MATT   Ronnie shuts up? That's gotta be worth something to somebody... I know... two drinks for Matt... make that a double... so that's... four drinks for Matt.

STAR   Something's up with Jimmy.

RONNIE   Why, what did he say?

STAR   I finally told him that I love him.

RONNIE   And what exactly did he say? I didn't quite get it.

STAR   *(mockingly)* "Ah? Ah? Yah... that's cool."

ZHANGWESH   What did he say?

MAA-IIN-GAHNS   "That's cool."

WASSEN   That's cool?

ZHANGWESH   What's... "That's cool?"

MAA-IIN-GAHNS   Will you guys be quiet. I can't listen to both worlds at once.

RONNIE   So what are you going to do?

STAR   What can I do?

> *JIMMY is now standing by MATT at the Life board.*

JIMMY   Ahhh... why the hell does this have to be so complicated?

MATT   Well it's not really... ahhh... here read these.

> *Hands JIMMY the instructions for Life.*

JIMMY   What the hell am I supposed to do now?

MATT   Well you get in these little cars and you build up your perfect little family and your dream job...

JIMMY   I gotta... I just gotta get out of here for a while.

MATT   Nah uh, not until you finish school, get a good job, and pay off your debts.

STAR   I don't think he's ready.

RONNIE   Ready for what?

STAR   To be with me... to be there *for* me... to just stick around for once, you know.

JIMMY   I mean, look at her! She doesn't even know what the hell she wants; she's just trying to keep me here!

MATT   You need a drink but you should never drink alone. It's a dirty job; somebody has to do it…. What about Matt? Matt, would you like to drink with Jimmy? Don't mind if I do.

JIMMY   "I love you, Jimmy…." What the hell did she think that stupid song meant! Screw this!

> *JIMMY leaves.*

STAR   I mean, I know what I want.

RONNIE   Well what?

STAR   Do I have to spell it out for everybody. I want him to be there FOR ME!!!!!!

RONNIE   Shouldn't you be there for him, too?

STAR   Whose side are you on?

RONNIE   I'm not on anybody's side, Star. This is Jimmy we're talking about—that's just how he is.

> *They sit for while and stoke the fire. Our attention goes to CHUCK and ANNE in the attic.*

CHUCK   *(at the height of passion)* I… I… I… love… youooooo!

MAA-IIN-GAHNS   Oh baby!

MATT   Chuck, you landed on a Life tile and it says… baby boy.

> *STAR goes to the now extremely intoxicated MATT who is still caught up in the board game.*

STAR   Where is everybody?

MATT   Well… *(He points her out on the board but coincidentally ANNE becomes visible at the exact time; adjusting herself, ANNE comes down the ladder and pours herself another mug of wine.)* there's Anne…. I guess Chuck's out now, too *(flicks the game piece off the board)* and Jimmy's been out of the game for a while. You know what? I don't think you guys are taking this game very seriously…

> *In the background, in the house, CHUCK, still in his boxers, goes up behind ANNE to hold her but she pushes him away. RONNIE, seeing this, is not very impressed.*

STAR   Well, where's Jimmy?

> *MATT looks around but does not see JIMMY anymore.*

MATT   Where is Jimmy? *(looking)* Wheeeeerrrsss Jimmy? Heeeeerrrrsss Johnny! *(referring to the bottle of Johnny Walker)* But wheeeeerrrrrsss Jimmy?

STAR   For fuck sakes, Matt! Sober up!

> *STAR makes her way toward the house. MATT goes to pass out on the bundle of stuff STAR carried in at the beginning of the scene. ANNE, CHUCK, RONNIE, and STAR come face-to-face, ANNE with the quilt in hand and CHUCK in his boxers.*

CHUCK   Oh… ahhh? Hey, Ronnie.

> *They look at each other; RONNIE is very upset, on the verge of tears. ANNE does not know that CHUCK and RONNIE have been seeing each other.*

ANNE   What? Did I miss something here? *(noticing CHUCK and RONNIE's expressions)* Oh my god! You have got to be kidding me. Ronnie, I didn't know…

RONNIE   *(extremely upset)* No no… that's cool.

ANNE   Ronnie, come on I'm sorry…. It didn't mean anything.

CHUCK   What?

ANNE   Oh come on, Chuck…. We were just fooling around.

RONNIE   Yah Chuck… that's something you should know a thing or two about!

> *RONNIE exits.*

CHUCK   Oh yah that's real cool.

ANNE   Why the hell didn't you tell me?

CHUCK   I didn't know…

ANNE   You're an asshole.

STAR   *(to ANNE)* Why did you guys go and do a stupid thing like that for?

ANNE   *(referring to CHUCK)* Okay I didn't do anything that any of the other girls in this place haven't done.

> *CHUCK, upset by this comment, takes his clothes and exits.*

STAR   What the hell do you mean by that? What do you know about it anyways; you don't live here! You're just a wannabe.

ANNE   Yah? Thank god I don't live around this place, Poke-a-hot-ass! You guys are messed up.

STAR   Well then why don't you just pack up your pretty little summer cottage and go back to your perfect little life in your perfect little world, Mrs. Pretty-in-Pink.

ANNE, obviously hurt, backs away from STAR.

ANNE   *(resigned)* Actually Star, you don't know anything about my world and I'm not the enemy. I just wanted you to have a nice housewarming, is all.

ANNE exits and JIMMY re-enters; they pass each other.

JIMMY   Hey Anne!

ANNE   Yah, Jimmy, Have a nice life!

JIMMY, still in a state of frustration, walks to the front door and finds STAR at the top of the stairs.

JIMMY   Okay I love you! Is that what you wanted to fucking hear! I love you, Star! *(leaving)* I'm not playing this stupid little game anymore, Star, not with you or anybody!

MATT   You were out a long time ago, Jimmy.

JIMMY   Shut the fuck up, Matt!

STAR   Yah that's it, Jimmy, just run away like you always do.... It's easy, right? Then you don't have to ever deal with anything!

JIMMY   You know what the saddest part about this whole fucked up situation is, Star?

They stand staring at each other.

(crying) I really do love you.

JIMMY exits.

STAR   GO THEN FUCK! I don't need you anyway! *(to herself)* Any of you... I don't need your broken promises... I don't need your stupid fucking gifts...

Throws the tape that CHUCK had given her.

And I sure as hell don't need your fucking friendships.

Throws the rock that MATT had given her and MAA-IIN-GAHNS goes and gets it and brings back.

About as useless as my fucking family.

Throws the quilt.

MATT *(offers up something he had found in the bundle he has been lying on)*
What about this? Do you need this?

STAR No!

MATT Oh I know, I know. *(He goes and grabs the Life game box and hands it to her.)* Throw this.

> *MATT starts throwing things too. The two can ad lib at this point. STAR, being very angry, is aggravated more by anything MATT says. MAA-IIN-GAHNS brings the rock to MATT.*

Hey what about this. Do you still want this?

STAR Umm. Yah that can stay. *(places rock on the porch)* But this? *(the wedding veil)* This has got to go.

> *Begins to realize that she doesn't actually need any of this stuff.*

You know what? This... all of this... I don't need any of this shit.... It can all go.... Put it back...

MATT Huh?

STAR Put it back... get it... get everything.

> *They begin gathering everything back up and place it in the bundle.*

This stuff? Is this me, Matt? Is this who I am?

MATT It's who you've been.

STAR Not anymore!

> *STAR grabs the bundle of stuff that she had been struggling with at the top of the scene, now with ease, and throws it down the side of the ravine. You see an obvious shift in her demeanour and physical presence as though the bag was all her burden. As the bag is flying through the air, STAR and MATT scream at the top of their lungs (howling) to which the wolves respond and howl back. As STAR turns around, she sees the wolves for the first time and reacts as though she had come across them in the middle of the forest and is startled but not frightened. MATT, on the other hand, does not see them and is wondering what STAR is reacting to.*

MATT What?

> *MATT passes out on his feet and falls to the ground. STAR turns around and sees him flat on his back. She goes to help him inside the house to pass out.*

STAR Geez, Matt, why do you have to get so drunk all the time?

Black out.

Interlude—1995–2005

The following interlude should be set to music. The music should set a sombre yet hopeful mood, a song about relationships, living, loving, leaving, reuniting. The cast members, along with the director, could determine the song. The following monologues were written by the original cast members in the show and can be used or the actors may substitute new monologues from their own point of view on their characters.

Facts that need to be included:

ANNE and MATT should have remained close friends throughout the years and both live in Toronto. ANNE now looks quite professional and writes for NOW *magazine.*

MATT, after a long struggle with his identity, is now openly gay and is in his clubbing outfit in downtown Toronto.

RONNIE has gone on to pursue formal education to the highest level and we see her in her graduation garb.

CHUCK is now a contractor with several kids. He is a single father.

JIMMY has been gone since the "incident" and has only remained in contact with CHUCK.

The monologues should be recorded and mixed in with the music. As each character's monologue is played they come on stage and we see them in their own environment. The recording is as though these thoughts are taking place in their head. There should be nobody else on stage except the actor during the monologues.

During the verses of the song, the stage crew comes out and again begins to transform the house to ten years later. The house is now condemned and empty.

*CHUCK   Look at this place. Fills my head with so many memories. Mostly good, but some bad, and some worse. I remember the exact spot where we first met. Not far from the exact spot where she broke my heart.

Yep, my first and only love. I've been with many girls—it just was never quite the same as being with Anne. Wooh! Just saying her name gives me butterflies. I saw her once on the subway; most nerve-racking two minutes of my life. I don't think that's ever happened to me with anyone else. Is that normal?

Wonder how Star's doing. Damn I miss that girl. The only girl brave enough to put me in my place and not give a shit.

Yep. Star and Jimmy kissing in a tree. K-I-S-S-... "yah that's cool." What an idiot. Well I guess we were all kinda idiots back then.

Well of course, except for Ronnie. Bet she turned out pretty good. I just loved those conversations that would go on and on and on and on.... Well maybe I didn't like them that much.

Wonder what ever happened to Matt. Now there's a messed-up character right there. Last time I saw Matt he was corked! Still the funniest guy I ever knew. Feel bad about teasing him all the time.

Can't be a prick all your life. Lost too many friends, family, and well, relationships, I guess. Just wish I could have salvaged the one that really mattered.

*MATT   Missing pieces... missing pieces of the puzzle, missing pieces of myself. So confusing. Feel more of a belonging in the city. I can be me. Totally. Living on the Rez, I felt as though I was running away from myself. I didn't want to lose my friends, so I hid myself, even from myself. *Mostly* from myself.

I remember standing in my washroom, looking in the mirror saying, "I'm gay," over and over again. And it still felt like I was hiding something.

I think I'm happier now. But I don't know how much longer I'm going to be able keep going to Zig's on Wednesday nights. It's a heck of a lot easier being accepted there than at home on the Rez. But I'm starting to feel like they accept me just because I am like them. My old friends at home accepted me even though I wasn't. The pact we made as kids was a lot stronger than I thought it was.

*Jimmy/Chuck Phone Conversation

CHUCK   Hello?

JIMMY   Hey Chuck! Chuck man, it's Jimmy.

CHUCK   Jimmy! Where the hell are you?

JIMMY   I'm in Singapore, dude. Hey listen, I need you to run to my mom's and tell her I'm coming home.

CHUCK   Are you? Well you got another reason to come home there, buddy. I'm having another kid.

JIMMY   Are you? Cool.

*Matt and Anne Computer Chat

ANNE   I know you're there, your status says online.

MATT   Sorry, chatting with dot dot dot someone else.

ANNE   Is he hot smiley face?

MATT   L-O-L big smiley face yah do you want me to send a jpeg of him?

ANNE   Not right now I'm jumping in the shower. I want you to call my cell before you head to the bar.

MATT   Okay be about an hour.

ANNE   Cool T-T-Y-L.

MATT   T-T-Y-L.

*RONNIE   It's not the same. Seems like when I'm with any of the old crew, at least one of us will say it at some point. "It's not the same."

Last time I heard it was from Star. And I guess she's right.

One summer when I was home from school, I went to the powwow. I ran into Anne and her mom. I said hi, just to be polite, and then she asked both of us girls to get her lemonade. You know one of those really good lemonades you get at a powwow. So we were headed over to the food line. More out of habit than anything, we walked in silence. Of course there was a line-up. So then we were just standing in the line-up in silence.

Then out of nowhere, Chuck's girls came up to us, and they were holding what appeared to be a small, dead raccoon. The girls obviously thought it was fine. We didn't want to be the ones to tell them the bad news... we looked at each other... we looked at the girls... we looked at the road-kill... and we looked around to try and find Chuck. Finally we spotted him and suggested the girls might want to go and show their new little friend to their dad. They ran off. And Anne and I burst out laughing at the absurdity of it all. And just like that, it was the same.

Mmm mmm... ...not the same... somehow... better.

*ANNE   Not right now. Really, I don't want to tell that story. I've told it so many times, at dinner parties, on dates, interviews. It helps to break the ice. "I hung out with some Native kids during my summers; we'd play cowboys and Indians and I'd always have to play the Indian." There's a laugh, there's the raised eyebrows of "You have *got* to be kidding me."

There's that look of awe you get when you say you used to vacation on a reserve.

Telling the story of how Matt and I first met. *(big smile)* Matthew. The little boy with the big eyes, dressed as a cowboy, coming to my rescue. My hero. My brave hero.

I'm turning them all into anecdotes that people love to laugh at. Everything I learned, everything I did… they're just words now. They're empty.

Friends forever. Those words popped into my head the last time I told one of my tales and everyone was laughing. I didn't. I felt sick; my stomach sank. I made that promise, too. I refused for so long to admit to myself that they were still a part of me, who I was, who I had become. Who that is now, I'm not so sure anymore. I've summarized everything and in return I turned myself into the punchline.

They weren't just stories. They were people who saw me, who accepted me, and helped create me. It was my reality, a reality that to some seems like a bedtime story about lifelong friends who lived in a huge house and spent their days chasing fireflies, slaying dragons, howling like wolves. It sounds a little too magical, doesn't it? No one wants the bedtime version anymore.

I'm sleepwalking through a world where everything has to be done faster and easier, stories get shorter, details get lost and no one notices.

I'm worth more than that. And so are they.

We deserve more than just a giggle over a martini. I don't want to become lost with the details.

I need to wake up.

And I need to get back to work; no cowboy can rescue me from my deadline.

STAR From: Starlee_77@hotmail.com. Subject: the clubhouse has been condemned

MATT Hey, everybody, *(to himself)* Hello, Star. *(back to computer)* I'm not really sure what this means to people, but just a note to let you all know that…

RONNIE …the clubhouse has been condemned by the band. *(to herself)* Ever those guys.

CHUCK And they are tearing it down towards the end of August. *(to himself)* Hey, I wonder if they need a contractor?

ANNE   I know it's a long way to travel for some of you, but this place has always meant a lot to me. *(to herself)* I wonder if Matt would be into going…

EVERYBODY   It would be nice to see you all again.

STAR   P.S. If anybody knows how to get a hold of Jimmy let him know too. Star.

ACT III

Condemned

Summer 2005. The clubhouse is now condemned with yellow caution tape all around it. It is empty except for the items that were there at the beginning. An old piece of wood is nailed to the door with the word "Condemned" written across it. The two old car seats are now moved downstage by the fire pit. A tent is set up on stage left; it is STAR's but she is nowhere to be found at the moment.

CHUCK enters alone and has his moment with the place. He starts to look inside the tent for STAR. MATT enters and sees CHUCK. This next interaction should seem distant between the two of them, never really getting to a place of comfort.

MATT   Hey, Chuck.

CHUCK   Look who it is. Matt, holy shit, how the hell are you?

MATT   I'm doing well, you?

CHUCK   Ahhh you know, can't complain. So this place is coming down, eh? Look at this place. I could of fixed it; it didn't have to be condemned.

MATT   Well Chuck… some things can't be fixed, you know… sometimes you just gotta let it go.

CHUCK   Oooohhh watching a little *Dr. Phil*, eh?

MATT   Yah. You watch it too.

CHUCK   Ahhh… I might have caught it a few times… between contracts, you know… watching the kids…. Have you seen Star? She must be here. *(indicating fire)*

MATT   Ah no, oh hey… I seen your name on the housing list.

CHUCK   Yah! I got one… first time I've ever been a priority… single father… two kids…. So ahhh… what's up with you?

MATT   I'm getting married.

CHUCK   No shit!

MATT   Just kidding.

CHUCK   You know… Matt… I was hoping I would run into you…. You know growing up and stuff… I spent a lot of time picking on you…

MATT   Don't worry about it, Chuck.

CHUCK   Well I just wanted to say… sorry.

MATT   Don't worry about it. *(pause)* I am seeing somebody, though.

CHUCK   Oh yah? That's cool…. Are you happy?

MATT   Yah, I am.

CHUCK   Well that's all that matters, I guess eh? Look I'm gonna have to get going here; gotta pick up the kids…. But listen, if you or anybody else wants to stop by and have a beer or something later… umm… I'll be home… so… ah yah.

> *CHUCK gives MATT an awkward hug. MATT is caught off guard, and stiffens up. CHUCK exits.*

> *MATT has his moment alone in the place, grabs his rock and places it by the fire, writes a note to STAR indicating CHUCK's offer to go to his place. MATT exits.*

> *From offstage we hear RONNIE and ANNE stumbling through the woods, laughing and unsure if they are on the right trail.*

ANNE   I can't believe you got us lost!

RONNIE   We're not lost. I know exactly where we are. Everything's just overgrown. See there's the clearing right there, oh ye of little faith.

> *They enter and go into their own world exploring the space, reminiscing.*

ANNE   This is weird.

RONNIE   Yah but… good weird.

> *ANNE and RONNIE go to the house and want to enter. They notice the yellow caution tape but can't resist the temptation to go inside.*

ANNE   I think it's against the law to cross these lines. Are you gonna hold this up for me or what?

> *RONNIE holds up the caution tape and they enter and make their way towards the "Condemned" sign.*

RONNIE   Yah if it's condemned it's probably not even safe to go inside. Are you gonna give me a hand with this or what?

> *They tear off the "Condemned" sign that is across the front entrance and go inside.*

ANNE   Wow I've been going over and over this moment since I got Star's email.

> *She takes a deep breath and breathes in the atmosphere as though trying to suck the memories out of the place. She walks around the space touching things and rubbing herself against the furniture.*

> *While they are in the house, STAR returns from gathering more firewood. A very old MAA-IIN-GAHNS, with a lot of urging, follows behind. STAR is dressed as though she had just come from a ceremony of some sort.*

STAR   Come on, girl! Let's go, Maa-iin-gahns! By the fire, come on!

> *Our focus shifts back to the two girls in the house; RONNIE's helping ANNE up the ladder. She is having a bit of trouble which leads to them breaking out in laughter.*

> *STAR hears this and goes to see who it is. She enters the house through the side door and sees the two girls midway up the ladder to the attic.*

What are you looking for, eh? Your virginity?

ANNE   Oh yah funny.

RONNIE   Oh my god, Star!

> *RONNIE and STAR are very excited to see each other and hug.*

STAR   I missed you guys; it's been so long.

> *ANNE and STAR hug and ANNE hangs on very tightly.*

Okay okay! You're choking me.

ANNE   It just feels so freakin' good to be back here.

> *ANNE continues exploring the place and finds a cigarette.*

Hey I found a smoke!

STAR   Oh yah there's been some kids that have been hanging around here.

RONNIE   Kids here, eh? Imagine that? So how you been?

ANNE   Yah, you have to tell us everything that's been going on. Come! Let's sit on the sun porch and have a smoke.

They make their way back outside and sit on the stair.

STAR   You smoke?

ANNE   Nope.

ANNE lights up the cigarette.

RONNIE   Only on special occasions.

ANNE   Look at you, Star! You're in a skirt.

RONNIE   The latest bush fashions, I see.

STAR   I just came from a ceremony, geez you.

The girls share a laugh.

RONNIE   So what's new?

STAR   Well not much to say really.... I've been spending a lot of time out here, lately. Things are good. So, *(to ANNE)* you seeing anyone?

ANNE   Yeah. My therapist. Regularly.

STAR   No seriously.

ANNE   Yeah. Seriously. I was seeing this guy. I thought he was kinda nice, but Matt didn't think much of him, and then Ronnie told me some of the things she had heard about the guy and from there we pretty much determined that he was crazy. So we broke up.

The girls share another laugh.

Remember that time Maa-iin-gahns fell through that chair by the fire and she was just stuck in the frame of that chair till we got back?

STAR   Or that time we caught Chuck in Ronnie's panties?

ANNE   Oh yah, he thought he was all alone and he was just dancing away. *(to RONNIE)* Did you ever get those back?

RONNIE   I didn't want those back!

The girls share yet another laugh.

Oh hey, I've got some news.

ANNE   What?

RONNIE   I'm moving back home.

STAR   You're kidding? What about your career and stuff?

RONNIE   Well, seven years of post-secondary and thirty-five thousand dollars in tuition fees later, I thought it was about time to come home and learn a few things from my mom. I don't know if you've heard but she's not doing so well these days.

STAR   Oh. I'm sorry to hear that.

ANNE   It's hard, you know, this whole growing old thing.

The dog wakes up and gets into a more comfortable position. ANNE and RONNIE notice MAA-IIN-GAHNS.

Maa-iin-gahns? Oh my god, that dog's still alive?

Heads over to the dog. RONNIE and STAR follow.

STAR   Speaking of old. I got a feeling this old girl's on her last legs.

Noticing the rock and the note left by MATT, STAR picks it up and reads it.

ANNE   What's that?

STAR   Matt's been here already. Says Chuck invited us all over to his place tonight, and that he'll probably head over later.

RONNIE   Yah that sounds like fun. *(to ANNE)* Think you can handle it?

ANNE   Ah shit yah… it's all water under the bridge. I'm just glad to be here… except for these flipping mosquitoes…. This is a part I didn't miss.

RONNIE   Yah, they always did like you…. Well we should get going before it gets any darker, if we're ever gonna find our way back. Are you coming, Star?

STAR   Yah… I'll catch up with you guys…. I need to take care of a few things here first.

RONNIE gives STAR a hug before she goes to leave.

ANNE   Okay well… we'll see you at Chuck's then…. Are you sure you're okay alone?

STAR looks at ANNE incredulously.

Oh yah? Right. 'K see you.

ANNE gives STAR a hug and the two girls leave. JIMMY enters but stays at a distance, out of STAR's sight.

STAR stokes the fire and sits down and has her moment with the place. She looks at the wolves.

JIMMY watches STAR from a distance.

STAR   Come here, Maa-iin-gahns, come here girl.

MAA-IIN-GAHNS makes her way over to STAR.

Did you ever hear the legend of the first dream, Maa-iin-gahns?

At this point in the story STAR goes on to tell the "Legend of the First Dream."

At the request of Cultural Advisor Eddie King this story has been altered from its original form in order to maintain the integrity of the oral tradition from which it came. The following is a summary by Joe Osawabine.

When the first child was born on earth the mother did not know how to care for it. The seven values—love, honour, respect, truth, trust, compassion, and patience—were watching from above and wanted so much to help. The creator told them they could help but could not interfere physically. The seven values then got together and devised a dream that they would send to the mother to show her how we, as humans, are to care for each other. And the dream simply stated, "Watch the wolves."

The legend in its original form is an important part of the story and should be told verbatim whenever possible. The legend can be obtained by contacting De-ba-jeh-mu-jig Theatre Group.

Did you know you're part wolf, Maa-iin-gahns? 'Cause you are. And you should be very proud of that. *(pause)* 'K go lay down! Go on! Go lay down.

STAR goes into the tent for something.

JIMMY makes his way towards the tent and looks around the space, contemplating whether or not seeing STAR would be a good thing and maybe on the verge of leaving.

STAR comes back out and sees him.

Well, well, well… look what the dog dragged in.

JIMMY   I don't think this dog could drag anything…

Awkward silence.

Uh… hi.

STAR   Hi.

They hug.

Ah? Let's sit.

They sit on the chair by the fire.

JIMMY   So? How are you?

STAR   I'm good, Jimmy. I've been spending a lot of time out here and well… it's given me a lot of free time to think.

JIMMY   Yah, I've had plenty of that myself.

STAR   Yah, you've been travelling, haven't you? Where you off to next?

JIMMY   No plans really, and you?

STAR   Ahh... I have a few ideas but...

> *Long silence to the point of discomfort. STAR stokes the fire.*

JIMMY   I'm sorry, Star.... This is too hard for me.

> *JIMMY gets up and goes to leave.*

STAR   Jimmy? You don't have to leave.

> *During this sequence all the lights are slowly fading down except for the light of the fire and the special on the wolves.*

> *JIMMY turns and looks at STAR. The audience should be unsure as to whether he will stay or leave.... JIMMY takes the backpack, unzips it and, as he is walking back, takes out a bottle of water. STAR goes to get a cup and hands it to JIMMY. JIMMY takes the cup, fills it, and hands it to STAR. They drink at the same time, JIMMY from the bottle and STAR from the cup.*

> ***In the Odawa culture, the marriage ceremony is carried out by an offering and acceptance of water.*

> *STAR notices the wolves again and sits and watches them.*

JIMMY   Star... I ah... I just wanted to say...

STAR   Shhh.... Do you see them? *(motioning towards the wolves)*

> *JIMMY and STAR both look for a long time at the wolves.*

You know they say if you watch the wolves, I mean really watch them, their packs, you know, that they display all of the seven teachings in everything that they do. Love. Honour. Truth. Trust. Respect. Compassion. And Patience.

JIMMY   Have they always been here?

> *STAR only nods her head in affirmation; they move closer together until they embrace.*

I missed you, Star.

STAR   I missed you too, Jimmy.

> *They embrace.*

> *The end.*

New Voices Woman

De-ba-jeh-mu-jig staff photo. Left to right: Bruce Naokwegijig, Anonghonse Kitchikake, and Joe Osawabine.

New Voices Woman was written by Larry E. Lewis.

New Voices Woman was first produced in 1993 by De-ba-jeh-mu-jig Theatre Group, with the following company playing various characters:

Levi Aguonie
David Assiniwe
Jeffrey Eshkawkogan
Gloria Eshkibok
Rona George
Francis Kaboni
Anonghous Kitchikake
Pamela Manitowabi
Shannon Manitowabi
Vince Manitowabi
Bruce Naokwegijig
Kristine Ominika
Joe Osawabine
Duke Peltier
Joshua Peltier
Adam Shawana

Directors:	Alanis King Odjig
	Alejandro Ronceria
Stage Management:	Jeffery Trudeau
Lighting Design:	Hugh Conacher
Sound Design:	Marsha Coffey
Set and Costume Design:	Linda Leon

Characters

MUDJEEKAWIS
      BEE #2
      SHADOW #2
      KINOZHAE

PAPEEKAWIS
      GIANT #1
      RATTLESNAKE
      LITTLE MAN SPIRIT
      SHADOW #3
      FROG WOMAN
      GREAT BLACK CATFISH

CHIBIABOS
      GIANT #2
      DEER WOMAN
      BEE #1
      SHAWDOW #2
      GREAT WHITE CATFISH

DEBAJEHMUD
      NOHNGOSE
      WATER LILY
      KINEU

NAMELESS ONE
      NEW VOICES WOMAN

GRANDFATHER (voice-over)

GRANDMOTHER (voice-over)

New Voices Woman

*The most important images of the play are Sun, Moon, Earth, Fire,
Water, and Air.*

*There is a fire burning at the side of the stage, and on it, a rabbit is
roasting. Four men enter: DEBAJEHMUD, a simple fellow, is
a storyteller. MUDJEEKAWIS is a wiry warrior. PAPEEKAWIS is
the fashion statement of his time, larger than life. CHIBIABOS,
a walking one-man-band, is making music.*

MUDJEEKAWIS   Stop that noise!

PAPEEKAWIS   If you stop making that racket, Chibiabos, I'll show you
what's hidden in my hands.

> *CHIBIABOS stops playing and looks at PAPEEKAWIS's hands. He
> opens his fists and shows him three plum stones.*

MUDJEEKAWIS   Ach! Nothing but plum stones!

PAPEEKAWIS   I could teach you how to gamble with them.

CHIBIABOS   I could show you how to make music with them.

> *CHIBIABOS grabs the stones, shaking them with a definite beat in
> a bark container, infuriating MUDJEEKAWIS, who grabs the stones
> and threatens to shove them down CHIABIABOS's throat.*

MUDJEEKAWIS   Or how about I kill you with them, Chibiabos!

PAPEEKAWIS   That might be more entertaining than listening to
Debajehmud talk.

DEBAJEHMUD   I'm a very good talker.

PAPEEKAWIS   You never know when to shut up.

DEBAJEHMUD   Fine, then. I won't tell my story, even though you play
a really important part in this one. Too bad.

> *DEBAJEHMUD prepares to leave, but PAPEEKAWIS stops him.*

PAPEEKAWIS   Okay, okay. Maybe you could just tell the part of the story
where I come into it.

MUDJEEKAWIS   No way would I let Debajehmud stick me in one of his
dumb stories.

DEBAJEHMUD   But you are in this one, Mudjeekawis.

MUDJEEKAWIS   You don't say.

DEBAJEHMUD   I couldn't take you out of it even if I wanted to, because then the story would be incomplete, and that would make it untrue. And I never tell what isn't true.

> *CHIBIABOS plays a quick trill of music.*

PAPEEKAWIS   Quit that, Chibiabos! You're making me crazy!

MUDJEEKAWIS   Your stories aren't real.

DEBAJEHMUD   The truth is as real as it gets.

> *MUDJEEKAWIS pushes DEBAJEHMUD and CHIBIABOS plays his music.*

MUDJEEKAWIS   Fight me. Beat me in a fight, and I'll believe anything you say.

DEBAJEHMUD   I couldn't beat you in combat, Mudjeekawis. But I know of one who could.

MUDJEEKAWIS   Let me at him! Let me at him! Who is this man who can beat me in battle?

DEBAJEHMUD   In hunting, too. But it isn't a man.

MUDJEEKAWIS   Not a man? *(reverently)* A spirit?

> *CHIBIABOS is completely lost in his music makers.*

PAPEEKAWIS/MUDJEEKAWIS   SHUT UP, CHIBIABOS!

DEBAJEHMUD   Neither man, nor spirit.

MUDJEEKAWIS   What else is there?

> *A young woman, dressed as a man, enters, carrying a slain beaver. This is NAMELESS ONE. MUDJEEKAWIS stands.*

Who made this kill? We will prepare the feast to honour the boy.

NAMELESS ONE   I bring the beaver to our village.

MUDJEEKAWIS   Why can't you be satisfied to be a woman?! You dishonour every boy here when you take a kill away from him. Look at you! Every day you become more like a man! Wild thing, what you need is a real man to tame you.

> *PAPEEKAWIS, still at the fire, turns to DEBAJEHMUD.*

PAPEEKAWIS   No man will love a woman who is a better man then he is himself. If I were a woman, I would be ashamed to look the way she does. If I were a woman, I would be the most beautiful, gorgeous, graceful and delightful creature on the face of the earth! Whatever I am—

man, woman, beast—I always tend to be a cut above the rest. For instance, if I were say—

DEBAJEHMUD   A skunk?

PAPEEKAWIS   That's not funny, Debajehmud. In fact, I think it's pretty rude.

MUDJEEKAWIS   Enough! (*to NAMELESS ONE*) Will nothing persuade you to stay home with your mother?

NAMELESS ONE   It is not in me to do it.

MUDJEEKAWIS   You need to be controlled, woman. For your own good. There is only one man who can do it. Me. You will be my woman.

NAMELESS ONE   How is a man to know my name when I don't even know myself who I am? He will call me what he wants me to be, then claim me, like a prize in a game. Let me seek for my direction on my own, through a vision.

MUDJEEKAWIS   You can't turn the moon into the sun. You are a woman, like a circle, whole and complete. A vision may only be sought by men. It has been decided.

> *MUDJEEKAWIS storms off and the men follow.*

NAMELESS ONE   Sometimes that circle is broken. There is something missing in me. Inside this flesh, beyond my bones... is there nothing but confusion and emptiness? No, not empty. Like a ball of fire, hidden so deep, I can't find it to fan or put out the flames. But the fire is blazing. The heat will rise in great waves, and I'll see then, I'll know. When that ball opens, will it be holding what is fine, what is strong? Or will it be evil, black, and wrong, and make of me a cinder, an ash ill-remembered. Whatever is there, I'm going to see. I'm going to touch it. No man will know me before I know myself.

> *She starts to run off, but two GIANTS (PAPEEKAWIS and CHIBIABOS), with holes where their hearts should be, enter. With them, there is a dancing flame (DEBAJEHMUD). NAMELESS ONE hides.*

GIANT #1   Did you kill them all?

GIANT #2   I ripped heads from shoulders and swallowed their blood. I chewed on their eyeballs and made myself so fat and lazy, I let a few get away.

GIANT #1   And those will be the ones who will destroy us, you idiot! You bloated fool! Can't you be trusted to do anything right?!

GIANT #2   You don't have to get mean about it. Geez. Anybody could make a mistake.

GIANT #1   Take all their food. When winter comes, the people who are left will starve, and we can pick up their carcasses next spring. *(to GIANT #2)* Make yourself useful. Grab that food.

GIANT #2   Boy, you sure are smart! Yup! That's what I always say! You're the smart one.

> *The GIANTS hobble out with the flame. As they exit,*
> *MUDJEEKAWIS sneaks over to the fire to eat.*

MUDJEEKAWIS   Nothing! They've left us nothing. We hunt, and this strange race of heartless giants steals our food. I fought with them, but they wouldn't die. Will nothing kill them?

> *NAMELESS ONE comes out of hiding.*

So, you're still alive, are you? We'll have to head into the setting sun, where the giants will never find us.

NAMELESS ONE   Run away? This is the birthplace of our fathers. Listen, there is a secret known to me. In a dream, I saw their village, far to the north, beyond the Great Lake. There, in their village, is a nest where the beating hearts of the giants are kept when they go on their raids. Destroy the hearts and the giants will die.

MUDJEEKAWIS   I will make that journey.

NAMELESS ONE   My dream tells me I'm the right one to do it. I have the skills. I have the strength!

MUDJEEKAWIS   It would take a great warrior to destroy the hearts of the giants. It would take a man.

> *With resolve, MUDJEEKAWIS exits.*

NAMELESS ONE   I will not be woman or man! I will be nothing in this world, because I was not meant for it. Let me serve the people, or let me die in the attempt.

> *She turns to find a hideous hag, DEER WOMAN (CHIBIABOS),*
> *dressed in blood-soaked rags of fur. Her feet are hooves.*

DEER WOMAN   You better have water and then food.

> *DEER WOMAN takes a leaf, crushes it in her hand, and pours*
> *water into NAMELESS ONE's cupped hands. Happy and surprised,*
> *she drinks as DEER WOMAN crushes a stone beneath her hooves*
> *and gives it as food for NAMELESS ONE, who eats it hungrily.*

Will you walk with me for a way?

NAMELESS ONE   I can't. I've got some giants to kill.

> *DEER WOMAN moves into the shadows, and RATTLESNAKE (PAPEEKAWIS) appears, coiled. NAMELESS ONE almost sits on him. He shakes his rattles. She jumps.*

Why are you rattling at me?

RATTLESNAKE   I have shed many skins. I am what I do, and what I do, I do very well.

> *She backs carefully away from the snake.*

NAMELESS ONE   I won't disturb you. I'll wait over here for my friend.

> *DEER WOMAN enters, searching for the girl. She has a forked stick in her hand. She sees the snake.*

DEER WOMAN   Hello, dear enemy.

RATTLESNAKE   The Deer Woman is not your friend. She is not a woman at all. She is a witch! She will steal your spirit away with her evil magic. Tell me, has she given you anything to drink?

NAMELESS ONE   Yes.

RATTLESNAKE   Tsk tsk tsk. And food to eat?

NAMELESS ONE   Yes.

RATTLESNAKE   That's bad, very bad. You poor thing! Quick! Hide down here in my caves with me, away from the sorceress!

NAMELESS ONE   But she's my friend.

RATTLESNAKE   No, no. That's only how she appears.

> *NAMELESS ONE is confused.*

DEER WOMAN   Friend?

NAMELESS ONE   Stay away. I am afraid of your magic.

RATTLESNAKE   That's the way. Closer, come closer.

DEER WOMAN   I see. I used my powers to help you, and now you turn on me and refuse my friendship?

NAMELESS ONE   I want nothing more to do with you or your powers. Your magic is as ugly as you are. I hope we never meet again.

> *She tears off the rag cape and throws it at DEER WOMAN's feet.*

DEER WOMAN   (*hurt*) Nameless One, we were great friends and companions, but not any longer. I could bring you to your knees…

RATTLESNAKE   She's a witch, didn't I tell you? Closer, come closer.

DEER WOMAN   ...but because we shared the medicines, I'll let you be. Call your fears, and they'll devour you. Nameless One, the Fear Caller. Nameless One, the frightened rabbit! Is that to be your name? Go to the snake, rabbit, if that's who you are! The sweet medicines that bound us are broken.

> *NAMELESS ONE backs up and turns, realizing she is almost within striking distance of the snake. DEER WOMAN moves away, but hovers in the shadows, watching.*

RATTLESNAKE   Come, I'll teach you the ways of the world.

NAMELESS ONE   No, Rattlesnake, no. I am afraid of you. The witch has made me afraid of everything.

RATTLESNAKE   You have reason to fear. The Rattlesnake slips over sand and rock, hunting for prey. He intends to make a feast of you.

NAMELESS ONE   What kind of teaching is that?

RATTLESNAKE   A final lesson.

NAMELESS ONE   What?! You're going to kill me?

RATTLESNAKE   I told you. I am what I do, and what I do, I do very well. A little closer. I have something to show you.

> *The RATTLESNAKE poises to strike, but DEER WOMAN moves between them, taking the venomous bite instead. She falls, but puts the beautifully decorated forked stick in NAMELESS ONE's hands. As the snake prepares to strike again, NAMELESS ONE traps its head in the fork of the stick.*

NAMELESS ONE   You fed me with lies about my friend because you intended to eat me. Creator, hear me now. My friend offered me drink and food and medicine and I did not remember to thank her. I remember now. I am not the Fear Caller, but the Woman With No Name. Thank you, Deer Woman. You do not know me because I have no name. But may my spirit always know you.

> *NAMELESS ONE slices the snake's head off with her knife. DEER WOMAN wraps the snake head in a piece of hide and gives it to NAMELESS ONE. The headless snake slinks into the shadows, and off. The lights fade into evening colours as NAMELESS ONE and DEER WOMAN take hands. The voice of a young woman is heard.*

NOHNGOSE   Walk the Shining Trail.

NAMELESS ONE   I don't know where to find it.

DEER WOMAN   It leads from earth skyward to a point beyond the farthest star. Step into the sky and walk the Shining Trail.

NAMELESS ONE   Will you come with me?

DEER WOMAN   No. The snake's venom is inside me now. I cannot heal myself, and you have no name yet to give you power. Go on your journey, friend.

> *As DEER WOMAN departs, there is a trail of tiny little star lights. NAMELESS ONE follows it. NOHNGOSE (DEBAJEHMUD), beautifully dressed, like a shimmering star, reaches out her hand to NAMELESS ONE and leads her carefully forward. NOHNGOSE breaks out of the freeze and goes towards the wings.*

NOHNGOSE   Papeekawis! Quick, or you'll miss your entrance. This is your best part!

> *PAPEEKAWIS hurries on, trying to struggle out of his RATTLESNAKE costume. He peers at NOHNGOSE.*

PAPEEKAWIS   Is that you under there, Debajehmud?

DEBAJEHMUD   Yes. Now hurry; the story has a life of its own and won't wait for us. Hurry.

> *DEBAJEHMUD quickly helps PAPEEKAWIS to change.*

PAPEEKAWIS   *(suspicious)* Am I a man at least?

DEBAJEHMUD   Yes, yes. Hurry.

PAPEEKAWIS   I'll use my deep voice, rich and resonating, shall I? Ohhhh, I'm gonna be so good! Watch every little move I make, Debajehmud; my performance will be perfection! *(He examines himself.)* Are you sure this is the right costume?

DEBAJEHMUD   Of course it is. Now, quickly! You start over there. Meet them on the Shining Trail and it's your job to make sure she never gets beyond the trail!

> *DEBAJEHMUD hurries back to the tableau with NAMELESS ONE, and freezes into position for a moment.*

PAPEEKAWIS   *(taking his position)* Not much of a costume, if you ask me.

> *He cartwheels towards them as the tableau unfreezes.*

Oh! It is a very athletic part, I see.

> *He blocks NAMELESS ONE and NOHNGOSE, and then somersaults. He does a pyramid, peering up at them from between his legs.*

NAMELESS ONE   What are you doing? *(to NOHNGOSE)* What is he doing?

LITTLE MAN SPIRIT   Seeing things from a new perspective.

> *He rolls and jumps to a crouching position, facing them.*

You can't get by me, you know. I am very wonderful and very handsome and very strong and I am also very smart. So turn back now.

> *NOHNGOSE gestures at a large beehive.*

NOHNGOSE   There is the way.

NAMELESS ONE   The beehive?

> *NAMELESS ONE turns her back on LITTLE MAN SPIRIT, bored, and brandishing a big stick, faces the beehive and lectures to it.*

Now listen carefully in there; these are hard lessons I have to teach.

LITTLE MAN SPIRIT   Whatcha doin'? *(to NOHNGOSE)* What's she doin'?

NAMELESS ONE   *(pretending to weep)* You've trapped me, Little Man Spirit! So I'm giving up my journey. I'll just try and make the best of things, and teach.

LITTLE MAN SPIRIT   Well, now you're talkin'! *(beat)* Teach who?

NAMELESS ONE   The little people in here.

> *LITTLE MAN SPIRIT ventures forward, curious, looking at the enclosed beehive and trying to find a place to see inside.*

LITTLE MAN SPIRIT   *(peering)* Who is in there? Let's get a look at them.

NAMELESS ONE   You can't see inside unless you're prepared to teach them.

LITTLE MAN SPIRIT   *(aside)* If I let her keep teaching, she'll win those little people over to her side, filling them with lies about me and then they will grow up, and I might be overthrown. On the other hand, if I were to teach them, I could tell them the truth about myself. Boy, you gotta get up pretty early in the morning to pull the wool over my eyes! *(to NAMELESS ONE)* I'm their teacher now!

NAMELESS ONE   Well, then, you'd better know it all. When it's feeding time, let the little ones know.

LITTLE MAN SPIRIT   How will I do that?

NAMELESS ONE   Hit the schoolroom walls with this stick until they all come out.

LITTLE MAN SPIRIT   Ohhhh! *(He leans in.)* How many times should I strike it, when the time comes to eat?

NAMELESS ONE   Just keep hitting it. They don't hear well.

> *NAMELESS ONE and NOHNGOSE duck down out of harm's way.*

LITTLE MAN SPIRIT   *(lecturing)* Well, little people, you'll learn much faster on a full stomach. That's the first lesson. Come out, come out, and we'll eat.

> *He bangs on the hive, but nothing happens. He bangs again, nothing happens. He gives it a mighty whack, and the whole thing bursts apart. Two big bees (MUDJEEKAWIS and CHIBIABOS) come out, chasing him. They sting him on the head, the feet, his hands.*

BEE #1   Destroying all our hard work, Little Man?!

BEE #2   Did you think we had nothing better to do than build another home?

> *The two bees both sting him on the bum and he screams.*

BEES #1 & #2   And let that be a lesson to you, Little Man.

> *The bees chase PAPEEKAWIS off stage. NOHNGOSE leads NAMELESS ONE towards the sun, which must have a very special light.*

GRANDFATHER   *(voice-over in Old Odawa)*
You will give new voices
You will extend the green
You will give new breath
You will give new branches.

NAMELESS ONE   I can't understand you, Grandfather.

NOHNGOSE   He speaks the old language; his words were given to him by the Creator. The Grandfather Spirit says that you will give new voices; you will extend the green; you will give new breath; you will give new branches.

> *NOHNGOSE kneels before the Sun and picks up a tobacco leaf.*

This is a tobacco leaf so that you may always remember your grandfather.

NAMELESS ONE   Thank you.

> *NAMELESS ONE slips it into her pouch, and a special light rises on the image of the Moon as they go toward it.*

GRANDMOTHER   *(voice-over in Old Odawa)* You shall see far; you shall hear far; you shall feel things not near; you shall sense things unmoved and unformed.

NOHNGOSE   Ah! Our grandmother says that you shall see far; you shall hear far; you shall feel things not near; you shall sense things unmoved and unformed.

> *NOHNGOSE kneels down and picks up a blue, glowing rock crystal.*

This is a healing stone, so that you may always remember your grandmother.

NAMELESS ONE   Thank you.

> *She takes the stone and slips it into her medicine bag. When she looks up, NOHNGOSE is gone and the lights have faded on the sun and the moon. She prays as CHIBIABOS, MUDJEEKAWIS, and PAPEEKAWIS enter as SHADOWS. They begin dancing, creating the lake. They speak in eerie voices.*

WATER LILY   *(voice-over)* Help me! I'm drowning in the lake! Help me, somebody, please!

> *NAMELESS ONE looks up, searching for the direction of the voice.*

SHADOWS #1 & #3   Do not listen.

SHADOWS #1 & #2   She will grab you.

SHADOWS #2 & #3   Do not listen!

SHADOWS #1 & #3   You must follow the Shining Trail across the water... the trail Grandmother Moon has made for you.

SHADOWS #1 and #2   Look ahead, and don't stray from the path.

WATER LILY   *(voice-over)* Will no one help me?!

SHADOWS #1, #2, #3   Do not listen.

NAMELESS ONE   Where are you? Call out to same now so I can find you. I want to save you, woman. I can save you, if you tell me where you are. Woman!

> *SHADOWS #1 and #2 speak softly, hypnotically, like a song, underscoring the words of SHADOW #3. They repeat, "She will grab you. She will pull you down," three times.*

SHADOW #3   Do not listen to the song. It is beautiful, but very dangerous. It calls you to a place from which you will never return.

> *WATER LILY's (DEBAJEHMUD's) head appears through a slit in the fabric of the water. She reaches out with her hand.*

WATER LILY   Have pity, have pity! My children will be motherless. Save me from this death, I beg of you, kind, loving sir!

> *NAMELESS ONE moves onto the water, and we see the spectacle of her drowning. We see the arms and hands of WATER LILY pulling NAMELESS ONE down. NAMELESS ONE resurfaces.*

NAMELESS ONE   *(gasping)* Stop! What are you doing?

> *WATER LILY reaches up her arms and tugs hard again. NAME-LESS ONE disappears, resurfacing in another place.*

I was trying to help you!

> *WATER LILY gives a mighty tug and NAMELESS ONE disappears. WATER LILY rises, majestic, through a slit in the water. There are shells in her hair and on her breasts. Her lower half is a magnificent fish tail. The eerie music becomes overwhelming.*

WATER LILY   Bewitching... tempting... my music deceives and lures good men of the earth into a watery grave... and this man I've caught will be the possession of Water Lily, Siren of the Great Lake, and he will be mine... beneath the shimmering surface of the lake... forever!

> *The music swells as the water rises and WATER LILY disappears. The SHADOWS exit. CHIBIABOS quickly tears off his Shadow costume, and walks upstage of the lake, trying to imitate the music of the Water Beings. He listens, but there is no response.*

CHIBIABOS   Water Beings! I make an offering of my music! Call to me and I will follow you into your caves and tunnels beneath the lake! Water Beings! Hear me! For never have I seen creatures more beautiful than you.

> *He plays his music again. MUDJEEKAWIS enters.*

MUDJEEKAWIS   Chibiabos! Living is serious business.

CHIBIABOS   My music is serious business.

MUDJEEKAWIS   Yeah, right! Like, for instance?

CHIBIABOS   It consoles the people you injure in the wars you love to make.

> *The haunting music of the Water Beings can be heard.*

Listen! Do you hear that melody? She's heard me and now she calls to me.

MUDJEEKAWIS   Snap out of it and listen to me. Courage makes a man. Are you a man or not?

CHIBIABOS   Name any danger.

MUDJEEKAWIS   Since Debajehmud is taking us to the depths of the lake, go down there and fight the Great Catfish! I can handle it, but I would like to see what you're made of, brother. Anyway, if you cannot do it, I will.

CHIBIABOS   Oh, that's low. Now you've made me angry.

> *CHIBIABOS hears the music again. He walks straight into the waters and is pulled under. He surfaces three times to gasp for air, and then he's gone.*

MUDJEEKAWIS   Now look what I've done! He's drowned for sure. Oh, it's just a story. But is it? What am I doing? I've got to save him! Chibiabos!

> *MUDJEEKAWIS pulls back the fabric with great difficulty, fighting with the waves.*

Chibiabos! I was just kidding!

> *MUDJEEKAWIS is by now revealing the underwater world.*

You are no match for the Great Catfish! Nobody is! Chibiabos.!

> *MUDJEEKAWIS looks and sees NAMELESS ONE lying at the base of a shimmering rock, where a large shellfish sits, closed. On another shimmering rock, with her back to us, is FROG WOMAN (PAPEEKAWIS). She is cradling CHIBIABOS. MUDJEEKAWIS tries to get across the water, but he can't. It's like a wall. He pushes up against it twice.*

Let me in! Let me into the lake! I want to help my brother! Let me in!

> *The beautiful music begins to swell.*

I'll find some way into the depth of the lake! You see if I don't!

> *And he storms off as CHIBIABOS rises and looks about at the fantastic underwater world.*

CHIBIABOS   Beauty and peace. This is where I was meant to live. And where is the gorgeous Water Being who pulled me to my fate? Where are you, loveliness? Yoo hoo!

> *FROG WOMAN, keen of spirit, but with the nose and eyes of a frog and terrible mats in her hair, turns and smiles a toothless, come hither smile and holds out her arms to CHIBIABOS.*

FROG WOMAN   Here I am, handsome! Give me a fat kiss!

CHIBIABOS   *(alarmed)* But there must be some mistake.

FROG WOMAN I heard your music, big boy, and you answered mine. Oh, lover man, we were made for each other. I will squeeze you good and tight, and I'll never let go!

> *She kicks back her fish tail and runs after him. He screams and runs off, pursued by her.*

CHIBIABOS Debajehmud, you set me up! I'll get you for this!

> *A gentler siren's song is heard as the large shellfish opens. WATER LILY unfolds herself and emerges from it. She is about to kiss her captive when NAMELESS ONE comes to her senses and startles her. NAMELESS ONE pulls back, prepared to attack.*

WATER LILY You needn't be afraid.

NAMELESS ONE What land is this?

WATER LILY You are in the caves of the sirens.

NAMELESS ONE And what shall I do in these caves of yours?

WATER LILY Live. I am Water Lily. They were my cries for help that you answered.

NAMELESS ONE You weren't in trouble at all! What do you want with me? Take me back to my people. You have no right to keep me here.

> *NAMELESS ONE moves angrily towards her, but is very weak. She falls, holding her stomach, struggling to rise.*

WATER LILY Poor, weak creature, you need food.

> *WATER LILY opens a beautiful shell basket and pulls out a handful of writhing black snakes.*

NAMELESS ONE No offence, but I cannot eat that.

WATER LILY But it is our greatest delicacy. Try it.

NAMELESS ONE Forgive me, but do you have any fish here?

WATER LILY Fish???!!! You eat FISH???!!!!! We'd better see the Great White Catfish before you go around getting yourself into trouble.

> *WATER LILY goes toward NAMELESS ONE as she strokes the air and an eerie melody begins, hypnotizing NAMELESS ONE. WATER LILY speaks in gentle terms.*

Some say there are no powerful female spirits. That is not true. The Great White Catfish is very powerful. Believe me.

> *KINOZHAE (MUDJEEKAWIS), a strong male Water Being enters.*

KINOZHAE   Well, isn't this a pretty sight? What's he, your catch of the day? Water Lily, we made a pledge to each other that we would marry. Each other!

WATER LILY   I have the right to claim a human being if I want.

KINOZHAE   I'm strong, powerful. I can protect you. And our family.

WATER LILY   But you aren't gentle as this one is.

KINOZHAE   He's nothing more than a boy. Let me feed him to the Great Black Catfish, and then we'll stop all this lunacy and get married.

WATER LILY   No! I am taking him now to her White Sister, who knows how to be kind. Kinozhae, we cared for each other once. So respect my wishes now, and don't try to stop me.

> *WATER LILY leads the hypnotized captive off. KINOZHAE grabs NAMELESS ONE by the arm. She is startled, and gets a good look at him. The music begins and NAMELESS ONE goes without a fight.*

KINOZHAE   In the lowest caves there are powers darker than you ever imagined, Water Lily. You have broken our vows, now let me make a new one. I offer my life in service to the terrible Dark Sister, if she will destroy your new dreams... and you, with them.

> *KINOZHAE exits, with dark and foreboding music surrounding him. This changes into the theme of the GREAT WHITE CATFISH, a theme of great dignity. WATER LILY and NAMELESS ONE enter, and then the GREAT WHITE CATFISH (CHIBIABOS) makes her entrance. She is a creature with a human torso, covered in shells, a fish from the waist down, and a glittering white cat's head, complete with sensational horns. Three small fin-like wings protrude from her right arm, two from her left. She looks feminine, but there is a strong masculine power to her every move. As she speaks the music comes to an end.*

WHITE CATFISH   I am aged in wisdom. I have a great knowledge, Water Lily. I know you like this human.

WATER LILY   Great White Catfish, do you have medicines that can make this human into a Water Being?

WHITE CATFISH   What does the human have to say for himself?

NAMELESS ONE   I wish to be returned to my people. I was brought down here under false pretenses.

WHITE CATFISH   But false pretenses are what we are all about! Silly boy! You don't belong to those people up there.

NAMELESS ONE   But how will I live down here?

WATER LILY   As my husband, of course.

NAMELESS ONE   I don't think so.

WATER LILY   You could learn to love me, I know you could.

NAMELESS ONE   You don't understand, Water Lily... there's something....

WATER LILY   What's wrong with me?

NAMELESS ONE   It's not you. It's me.

WHITE CATFISH   You must marry the Water Being who brought you here and you must father many children.

NAMELESS ONE   That's... impossible.

WATER LILY   *(hurt)* You really don't want to marry me?

WHITE CATFISH   If you don't marry her and father many children, you will be catfish food.

NAMELESS ONE turns to WATER LILY.

NAMELESS ONE   You are a very beautiful person—I mean fish—well, whatever you are, you're pretty. But I am not going to marry you and that's final. What do you want with a homely guy like me?

WHITE CATFISH   Grind him up and we'll feed him to my Black Sister. She lives only on human flesh and blood. She's a nasty creature and she makes no end of trouble for me, as well for everybody else, but she gets lazy when she eats. A meal like you might appease her for a time, and give the rest of us a little peace.

Suddenly, there is an explosion of sound, like instruments crashing into each other. We hear the echoey, underwater voice of CHIBIABOS (recorded).

CHIBIABOS   *(voice-over)* Nameless One, run! It's your only chance.

NAMELESS ONE runs off in the direction of the voice.

WATER LILY   You let him get away.

WHITE CATFISH   You cannot hold what will not be held. Water Lily, my pet, another fate awaits him and his friend. He can't rise up into the sunlight shallows of the lake, for that is my domain and I'd catch him. There is nowhere for him to go but down, down, DOWN into the jaws of my Black Sister. I do wish she would get over her habit of eating them while they are still alive. The screams disturb my dreams.

Left alone on stage, WATER LILY makes a prayer.

WATER LILY   Hear a maiden's cry. I pray to every power of the deep to bring the human back safely to me. And when he returns… let him love me.

WATER LILY exits and dim, greenish lights isolate KINOZHAE.

KINOZHAE   A little deeper, Kinozhae. Have courage and go deeper, to the caves where no light ever shines. Spirits, make my heart as black as the waters I seek. If I cannot have Water Lily, then no one will have her!

We hear slow, asthmatic breathing. In the darkness, two huge red slit-eyes can be seen, the eyes of the GREAT BLACK CATFISH.

Do not kill me, for my service to the Black Sister will be great.

BLACK CATFISH   *(voice-over)* My jaws ache to rip those arms from their sockets. Ohhhh, it's been too long since I've heard the sweet music of my victim's screams.

KINOZHAE   Listen to me, Great One. I come to serve you. I am but half a meal, when I know in these waters there are two full human men to be had. Let me bring them to you, and you can feast.

BLACK CATFISH   *(voice-over)* I don't believe, not for one moment, that you have the power to bring me such a feast. Let me sting your heart.

KINOZHAE   On purpose?

BLACK CATFISH   *(voice-over)* I cannot kill you if your heart is black enough, and unless it is, you are no use to me. Then I'll split you, limb by limb, and eat you. The choice is yours.

KINOZHAE   Some choice. Very well.

KINOZHAE presses his heart against the red eyes and is shocked. He flies back and stays still. Finally, he gets to his knees.

BLACK CATFISH   *(voice-over)* When you are stung you become my slave. Fool! Know what it is to surrender completely to another, especially when she's as lowdown nasty as I am. Bring me your Water Lily, and the humans will follow. Ohhhhh! What a scrumptious banquet!

KINOZHE moves like a zombie, holding a knife in his hand. Behind him, the eyes of the CATFISH disappear. Breathless, CHIBIABOS and NAMELESS ONE enter. KINOZHAE slowly begins to move in behind them, knife raised.

NAMELESS ONE   But who are you?

CHIBIABOS   A friend in the same kind of trouble as you.

NAMELESS ONE   Our problems are not the same, believe me.

CHIBIABOS   We were dragged into these caves and we have to marry the Water Beings, or become lunch. I'd say we have a thing or two in common.

NAMELESS ONE   I can't marry a woman who is half fish.

CHIBIABOS   Would you want to marry a woman at all? Being a woman yourself, I mean.

NAMELESS ONE   How did you know?

CHIBIABOS   I've been following the story.

NAMELESS ONE   Tcht! If the Water Beings discover I am not what I seem, they will kill me, as sure as we're sinking to the bottom of the lake. But you! You could marry the Water Being, and father the children they need, and escape the terrible death that awaits me. You are a man!

Just as KINOZHAE is about to stab NAMELESS ONE, FROG WOMAN calls and her eerie music plays.

FROG WOMAN   *(voice-over)* Oh handsome man!!!

CHIBIABOS   Run!

They run, just narrowly missing the blade of KINOZHAE's knife. CHIBIABOS and NAMELESS ONE find a place to hide. Their attention is on FROG WOMAN, so they do not see KINOZHAE again moving in their direction. FROG WOMAN enters.

FROG WOMAN   Oh handsome man? I am waiting for you with my arms wide open. Won't you come and let me please you? Oh handsome young man, where are you? Where are you, my little wriggly-worm?

She runs off, searching.

CHIBIABOS   That is my betrothed.

NAMELESS ONE   She seems very willing.

CHIBIABOS   Way too willing, if you ask me. So, it is agreed. We'll stick together and help each other, no matter what comes.

NAMELESS ONE looks up. She sees KINOZHAE moving very close to them, knife raised. She can't speak. She elbows CHIBIABOS.

Not now. I'm keeping a lookout.

She elbows him again.

What is it?

He turns and sees KINOZHAE. They both holler and run again, just missing the strike of KINOZHAE's blade. They go offstage.

WATER LILY and FROG WOMAN drift on, from opposite sides.

FROG WOMAN   You look just as depressed as I am, Water Lily.

WATER LILY   I have troubles, too.

FROG WOMAN   Oh, spare me. You're pretty and feminine; you smell good. What kind of troubles could anyone as perfect as you are—in every way—possibly have?

WATER LILY   I caught a human this morning, and I took him to the White Sister so that we could be married. And he… he ran away from me!

WATER LILY begins to cry.

FROG WOMAN   No kidding? He must've been a crazy man to run away from a great beauty like you. As for me, no man or fish will ever want me. It's been that way since the day I was born. I even frighten the frogs. Maybe I should just end it all right here and now!

WATER LILY   Well, if you feel like that, go get eaten by the Dark Sister, and bring somebody joy.

FROG WOMAN   Don't make me laugh; I want to be miserable. Look at this face? Have you ever seen anything uglier? Be honest with me, now.

WATER LILY   Frog Woman, real beauty comes from within. Beauty like mine attracts them, but it doesn't always hold them. You know the music you create is by far the finest of any sound a Water Being has ever made. That music is your inner beauty. Bedazzle your man with it.

Suddenly she sees KINOZHAE coming towards her.

Kinozhae! Why are you raising your knife to me? Kinozhae! I'm Water Lily. Don't you know me?

As KINOZHAE prepares to strike, FROG WOMAN pushes WATER LILY out of the way. She falls and bangs her head on a rock. As WATER LILY struggles to her feet, dazed, FROG WOMAN beats her fists on KINOZHAE who stabs her in the heart. Blood spurts; KINOZHAE lifts WATER LILY into his arms and takes her offstage. CHIBIABOS enters with NAMELESS ONE. They see FROG WOMAN, and CHIBIABOS prepares to run in the opposite direction, but NAMELESS ONE stops him.

NAMELESS ONE   Chibiabos! She's hurt!

NAMELESS ONE hurries to her and FROG WOMAN slips to the ground. CHIBIABOS approaches.

CHIBIABOS   Who could have done such a thing?

FROG WOMAN   It was Kinozhae. His heart has been turned black by jealousy. Never mind about me. I'm not worth much of anything. You must hurry; find the caves of darkness where the Black Sister lives. Kinozhae has taken Water Lily there.

CHIBIABOS   We can't just leave her here.

NAMELESS ONE   We'll find a cave, and hide her. I'll leave you with my medicine bag. I don't know how to use it, but maybe the medicines will work for you. It's all I can offer.

NAMELESS ONE slips her medicine bag over FROG WOMAN's head. CHIBIABOS takes FROG WOMAN's hand.

CHIBIABOS   Get well, for I'm just beginning to see how lovely you really are, Frog Woman.

FROG WOMAN   I'm not lovely. I'm ugly. As I lie dying, there is only one thing for me to give. Hold me close to you, handsome man. And I will let my music pass through me into your heart. Hold me, just once.

CHIBIABOS holds her close. The music is astounding. CHIBIABOS helps her up, and he and NAMELESS ONE lead her off to a cave. From another direction, KINOZHAE brings WATER LILY onstage. She is coming to, and he puts her down, binding her hands behind her back with waterweeds. Then he binds her feet.

WATER LILY   Kinozhae, what are you doing? I have never harmed you!

KINOZHAE   But you have! You have harmed me!

WATER LILY   When we made our pledge, we were children. You were always good to others, Kinozhae, and as we got older, I thought I could learn to love you. And I did… until I saw the human on the shores of the Great Lake. When I saw him… I knew that there was a difference between the love I felt for you—the love of friendship—and the powerful love you feel only for a mate.

KINOZHAE   The kindness that lived in me has been eaten. Now, I serve the great, hideous monster of the darkest caves in these waters. You're my bait, to lure the humans into her lair. When they've been captured, she will devour you. I'll watch. And I won't feel a thing.

WATER LILY   Did I ever know you? You yellow-eyed monster, made sick with resentment, and anger, and rage…. Do you throw the goodness of your spirit away so easily? If that's so, you aren't the Kinozhae I once knew. Maybe my Kinozhae never was at all.

KINOZHAE   Stop! No more! You won't make me weaken. You aren't strong enough to break the ties that bind you, nor the ties that bind me to the ruler of the pitch black dead of night.

NAMELESS ONE and CHIBIABOS enter.

NAMELESS ONE   Let her go! Let her....

But NAMELESS ONE is distracted, and frozen, by what comes next.

The lights grow darker and the bloated BLACK CATFISH (PAPEEKAWIS) enters, slowly. Her entrance could almost be funny, if she weren't such a terrifying sight. Her eyes are red and filled with puss, and the horns on her head are twisted and curled, like the horns of a ram.

BLACK CATFISH   I'm hungry. But I'm not sure if even I can swallow so many succulent morsels in one sitting. Who will I dismember first? Let's have a fight. I'll eat the loser first.

KINOZHAE   Let me fight the man who poisoned Water Lily's heart with love. Let me fight him!

BLACK CATFISH   Idiot! You're one of mine.

KINOZHAE   If I win, let me be your second in command. And if anything ever happens to you, I will become the ruler of the deep.

BLACK CATFISH   Oh, that's good. That's very good. If you win, then I'll have to be watching my back every minute, because you'll be trying to kill me, to steal my power. Oh, I like it, I like it. It'll be the most fun I've ever had.

NAMELESS ONE   If I win, feast on Kinozhae, and upon me, if you must. But let Water Lily go.

BLACK CATFISH   All right. Listen would you mind if I chewed on your friend while you fight? The plump, delectable little thing.

CHIBIABOS   Does she mean me?

NAMELESS ONE   I'm afraid so.

CHIBIABOS   You know, Great Black Catfish, I'm not as plump as I look.

NAMELESS ONE   No. If I win, you must let him go. You may feast on me and on this Kinozhae if you must, and may I stick in your throat and choke you.

BLACK CATFISH   You're a nasty little thing. Very well. I'll wait. Fight!

The fight begins, very acrobatic, with NAMELESS ONE nearly losing. The GREAT CATFISH cheers, clapping with pleasure from time to time, leaning forward intently at other times. Finally, NAMELESS ONE flips KINOZHAE and puts the knife to his throat.

KINOZHAE Finish me off.

NAMELESS ONE I have won?

KINOZHAE With honour.

NAMELESS ONE Then let her take your life, for I have no need of it.

BLACK CATFISH *(clapping)* Very good, very good. I don't know when I have enjoyed myself this much. The problem is, I over-excited myself so much that now I'm really hungry. I think I will eat you all after all. Except my precious Kinozhae. I like his looks. I think we'll make babies together. Then I'll eat him.

KINOZHAE Yuck!

NAMELESS ONE That snapped him to his senses.

> *While BLACK CATFISH smacks her lips, KINOZHAE and NAMELESS ONE untie WATER LILY, then KINOZHAE throws his knife at CHIBIABOS's feet.*

KINOZHAE As you have both been honourable with me, I offer my knife. Chibiabos, pick up the knife before it is too late!

CHIBIABOS I am not a fighter. I do not make war.

NAMELESS ONE Water Lily, go to the caves of tenderness at the edge of darkness. You'll find Frog Woman there, and she needs you so.

> *WATER LILY and KINOZHAE exit hurriedly.*

BLACK CATFISH Oh, what a feast. I'll save the fingers and toes for last. They're my favourite little treat. Except for the tongues. Now then, which one first? Decisions, decisions! Bring me the chubby, juicy one first.

> *She plucks the air with her blade-like fingers as though strumming a harp, and awesome music lures CHIBIABOS toward her. He fights to stay back, but the music is too strong.*

Beautiful music, is it not? Who do you think created the music of the Water Beings? I did. And I gave it to them to lure fools like you into the darkness of my world so I could put you in my stomach. See how big my belly has grown? But there's always room for more. I hunger for bone-heads drunk on music.

NAMELESS ONE Chibiabos, remember your true gifts. Remember the power of your own music and mix it with the melody Frog Woman gave you, from her heart to your own!

> *CHIBIABOS takes up his flute, playing a counterpart that is achingly lovely and gentle. The music of the catfish goes out.*

BLACK CATFISH   What weapon is this? You filthy little pig, put that thing down... at once!

> *She sets her jaw, and plucks the air with each finger until higher, heart-searing music fills the air, driving CHIBIABOS to his knees. He summons all his strength and retaliates with trills so detailed, sustained, and then fantastically rapid that she is dazed into silence. A spotlight shines suddenly on the BLACK CATFISH. She screams and moves as quickly as she can out of the light, and all is darkness again. She cowers in the shadows, but the light finds her again and she screams. This time, no matter where she runs, the light follows her.*

What are you doing to me?!

NAMELESS ONE   Summoning your Light Sister, shameless one.

> *WHITE CATFISH (now played by DEBAJEHMUD) appears.*

WHITE CATFISH   Go down to your black hole and never come back, you dishonourable wretch. I'm ashamed to say you're my sister.

BLACK CATFISH   You have no power here. The darkness of the bottomless lake belongs to me.

WHITE CATFISH   Then let me flood it with light and drive you further down.

BLACK CATFISH   Let me fill your spirit with dark and let me drive you from the lake all together.

WHITE CATFISH   Sister, sister, that you can never do. You are my twin; you make me whole. And I complete the circle for you. We are one, black and white. Without the balance we make, there would be only chaos in the lake.

BLACK CATFISH   How did you get down here? HOW?!!!

WHITE CATFISH   Your lies, your cheating, and your dishonour called me down. When the Great Sisters, black or white, give their word, they keep it. You didn't. And here I am.

> *The stage begins to fill with light, slowly.*

BLACK CATFISH   The light will destroy me! You are my sister! My twin sister! Does family mean nothing to you? Why turn the power of light against me, your own flesh?

WHITE CATFISH   Dive deeper, sister, deeper, and save yourself from the light. Come, I'll go with you and see you safely into your blackened pit.

> *She takes her sister's hand and leads her off. BLACK CATFISH is snivelling.*

BLACK CATFISH   I don't see what's the point of being the bad one if you can't lie and cheat once in a while. I mean, I'm *supposed* to be bad.

WHITE CATFISH   There, there. Of course you are.

> *They exit, leaving CHIBIABOS and NAMELESS ONE alone on stage.*

NAMELESS ONE   You know, you did very well in your battle with the Black Catfish.

CHIBIABOS   It's kind of you to say so.

NAMELESS ONE   But it wasn't your power alone that defeated her.

CHIBIABOS   No. No, I guess not.

NAMELESS ONE   Of course, Frog Woman was a worthless being. She wasn't pretty at all.

CHIBIABOS   There are things that are more important than that. All she had was her melody, and she gave it to me. That's beauty! Of spirit!

NAMELESS ONE   It's true. Of course, she didn't really care about her music, did she? So I guess it wasn't a great sacrifice, or anything.

CHIBIABOS   She did so care about her music. She cared about it more than anything in the world.

NAMELESS ONE   Well, we don't need her anymore, do we? So let's find our way back to land, shall we?

CHIBIABOS   Boy, you can be ruthless when you want to be.

NAMELESS ONE   Oh, don't be sentimental. Frog Woman gave what she had and now, for all we know, she's dead and gone.

CHIBIABOS   No, don't say that! She has so much.... Without her, I'll never have the heart to make music again. What are we thinking of? We've got to find her. We've got to make her well.

NAMELESS ONE   It sure takes you long enough to come to your senses, Chibiabos.

> *KINOZHAE and WATER LILY lead the wounded FROG WOMAN onto the stage. They put down WATER LILY's shell cloak and FROG WOMAN lies on it. NAMELESS ONE kneels down and takes her gifts from her medicine bag. She puts the snake head above FROG WOMAN's head; she prays over the tobacco and scatters it at FROG WOMAN's feet; then she passes the glowing blue crystal over FROG WOMAN's heart. And FROG WOMAN, after a moment, rises.*

FROG WOMAN   Who are you?

NAMELESS ONE   I am Nameless One.

FROG WOMAN   That isn't a name to carry so great a spirit. Your kindness to me gives me power to return you to land, if that's what you wish.

NAMELESS ONE   Yes.

> *FROG WOMAN helps her gather up her medicines, returning them to the medicine bag.*

FROG WOMAN   The Great Sisters, Black and White, give you the gift of the plants of knowledge. You will always know where to find the medicines you need to heal your people. And may your people always come to you when they have need.

> *FROG WOMAN sprinkles some herbs into NAMELESS ONE's pouch.*

KINOZHAE   Just a minute! You can't send him back without Water Lily's approval, because she's the one who brought him down here. She loves him. She'll never let him go.

WATER LILY   I don't know, Kinozhae. I've seen many sides of you, more than I ever saw before. Some I don't like so much, but they make you… fuller, somehow. A little more real. A lot more loveable. I grant my permission to send the human back to the earth.

NAMELESS ONE   Well, that's a good thing. I couldn't father any of your children, you see, because… well, because I am really a woman, and I need to seek my path alone for a time yet.

WATER LILY   You're a woman?!

KINOZHAE   Impossible. You fight like a man.

CHIBIABOS   *(smiling)* She fights better than some men.

WATER LILY   I made a mistake? But I watched you. I watched all you did on the land. On misty mornings I would sit on the rocks, and I could see you hunting… a perfect man.

NAMELESS ONE   Appearances deceive.

FROG WOMAN   Pull yourself together. Chibiabos, I suppose I'd better send you back to land, too.

CHIBIABOS   Not if I can stay down here with you.

FROG WOMAN   But I'm so awful to look at!

CHIBIABOS   Not to me.

He kisses her on the lips, gently. Steam almost rises out of her ears.

FROG WOMAN   Well, gol-ly!

NAMELESS ONE   But Chibiabos…

CHIBIABOS   The Water Being has always been inside me.

NAMELESS ONE   But your music, your music! What will we do on earth without your beautiful music!

CHIBIABOS   It will always be there. Listen for it in the wind.

> *CHIBIABOS and FROG WOMAN go off together one way, KINOZHAE and WATER LILY in another. NAMELESS ONE stands alone, as the lights become red all around her.*

NAMELESS ONE   What fresh new torture is this for me? Let me alone! I am not strong! I have used all my strength to get here, and now that I'm finally in the den of the heartless giants, I haven't a drop of fight left in me! I thought I was rock. I believed I was hardbodied, that my stamina would never leave me while my resolve held. They were right! The people of my village were right! They held the truth between their teeth all along! I have always been unworthy. Let the snows fall from the sky and cover my arrogance, hiding my shame from the world. Let me never see another spring.

> *She sinks down in despair, and covers herself with a white cloth of snow, as KINEU (DEBAJEHMUD), badly wounded, crawls on.*

Kineu… from my old village…. Kineu? But you've burned yourself.

KINEU   I have been in the village of the giants. I crept in at night while they slept. I speared deep into the centre of one of the beating hearts in the nest, and it shot slime and ooze, and the stuff burns you like flames. They cannot be killed. I'm dying, Nameless One. Turn back or they will kill you, too.

> *The theme of the GIANTS is heard. The CHIEF GIANT enters, followed by two dancing flames, bearing the bowls of pulsating hearts. He comes toward the enemy.*

Thunder 'n lightnin'! Look at the size of that thing!

NAMELESS ONE   Come through the fire. Breathe strength into your body and move through the flames!

> *She grabs KINEU by the hand and they run, with difficulty, through the angry flames. NAMELESS ONE rubs on her medicine bag hard and then smooth, over and over. Then she reaches in and withdraws crushed herbs of knowledge. She leans carefully over the hearts and sprinkles the herbs over them. She picks up a heart and shows it to*

> *the gasping GIANT, who backs up. She puts the heart back in the bowl.*

Great Monster, your head is swollen with plans of conquest, dreams of killing, and stealing from the dead. The people you spare die more slowly starving for the food they have found and lost to our thievery. Take your heart, Giant. Slip it back into your chest. Let the blood flow through it; let it transform the lustful greed in your mind with its purity of purpose: life. Take back your heart, Giant. Or I will stand before you and eat it raw myself, and then I will show you no more mercy than you have shown my people.

> *The GIANT growls, furious, and takes an aggressive step towards her. KINEU, without much confidence, holds up his spear.*

KINEU   Are you crazy?!!

> *NAMELESS ONE takes up the heart and makes as if to take a bite of it. The GIANT does a little dance, whimpering and howling.*

NAMELESS ONE   Well? What's it to be?

> *The flames come forward cautiously, looking back at the GIANT who nods his head in resignation. They look at each other, shrug, and take the heart from NAMELESS ONE, slipping it into the hole in the GIANT's chest. The flames dance around the GIANT as they start to exit, and bang into one another. The GIANT points towards the other hearts. The flames, feeling foolish, run over to the bowl, and bear it off stage.*

KINEU   Not a single drop of blood was shed; yet you have won.

NAMELESS ONE   Respect for all beings. Go now, Kineu. Allow me to be myself, and maybe I will show you who I am.

> *We hear the music of the GREAT CATFISHES and KINEU moves respectfully off.*

GREAT CATFISHES   (*voice-over*) Neither one of us lives without the balance of the other; the dark and the lightness of being within you, girl. Earth, wind, water, and fire know you. Do you know yourself?

> *NAMELESS ONE finds her song and sings it for the first time. It is her discovery of self-knowledge.*

NEW VOICES WOMAN   I am Woman with powers to heal and to see into the future. Meegwetch for your gifts. And for my vision.

> *DEBAJEHMUD enters, with PAPEEKAWIS and MUDJEEKAWIS.*

MUDJEEKAWIS   Great story. I almost believed this one.

PAPEEKAWIS   Myself, I'm exhausted. I work my tailbone off, and that snip of a girl gets all the glory! Where is Chibiabos? Is he clowning around behind the scenery? *(calling)* Chibiabos! Chibiabos! Come out now. The story is over.

MUDJEEKAWIS   Where is he?

DEBAJEHMUD   Under the water in the lake, my friends. I told you when we began. I only tell tales that are true.

> *DEBAJEHMUD starts to go off, then turns and smiles, looking at NAMELESS ONE. PAPEEKAWIS is looking under sticks of wood, everywhere, calling for CHIBIABOS.*

MUDJEEKAWIS   Who is she? *(He approaches her.)* Who are you.

NEW VOICES WOMAN   I am New Voices Woman.

> *MUDJEEKAWIS embraces her, like a respected friend.*

MUDJEEKAWIS   Welcome, New Voices Woman. Welcome.

PAPEEKAWIS   Chibiabos, I know you're there. Chibiabos!

> *We hear the wind, and everything freezes until we hear a strain of CHIBIABOS's melody.*

> *The end.*

The Gift

The Gift is an original creation based on traditional teachings from the Odawa Midewin Lodge, provided by Eddie King.

The Gift was first produced in 2003 by De-ba-jeh-mu-jig Theatre Group, with the following company:

Creation Team:
Teodoro Dragonieri
Eddie King
Joe Osawabine
Elisha Sidlar
Jimy Sidlar-Bebonang
Bill Webster
Paula Wing

Peformers:
Joe Osawabine
Elisha Sidlar
Jimy Sidlar-Bebonang

Director:	Joe Osawabine
Stage Management:	Jackie Carpenter
Set Design:	Ron Berti
Costume Design:	Bill Shawanda
Original Music:	Elisha Sidlar
	Jimy Sidlar-Bebonang

Characters

JOE—A young man in search of his identity and relationship to his culture. This story is told through his point of view.

ELISHA—MUSE #1—helping the young man through his journey and providing musical interjections.

JIMMY—MUSE #2—also helping the young man through his journey and providing musical interjections along with Muse #1

De-ba-jeh-mu-jig staff photo. Left to right: Jimmy Sidlar, Joe Osawabine, and Elisha Sidlar.

The Gift

The stone structure of the Holy Cross Mission Ruins in Wikwemikong, Ontario provided the backdrop for the original version in 2003. Within the ruins was a low, raised stage platform surrounded by a backdrop of six fresh cedar bough panels. Downstage centre, between the audience and the stage platform, a fire burns. The petroglyph (a carving or inscription in rock) symbols for the Foundation Teachings are depicted on pieces of deer hide and are hung on each of the cedar bough panels. The ideal set-up would be situated on the ground with the audience sitting on the ground or on stumps as though sitting around a campfire. The Gift was also performed within a fifty foot tepee with the audience sitting in the round on blankets with the fire burning in the centre of the tepee.

JIMMY and ELISHA enter singing "What does it mean?"

Song "What does it mean?"
Written and performed by Jimmy and Elisha Sidlar.

What does it mean?
To begin again

Once upon a time a story was told
Live and in the flesh about a lifetime to unfold
Their eyes are on the box now real TV and gold
Happy ever after is sold without a moment's peace

What can it mean?
What can it mean?
When the wind wrestles through the trees
Does it remind you to remind me to breathe?

Not so long ago we walked on the moon
We staked out the best views of the earth in mid June
Our eyes are on the box as we bring the orb to ruin
Happy ever after comes too soon
Without a moment's peace

What can it mean?
Is the earth infinite until I'm lowered into it?

Not so far away a steel bird flew right into a tower
What a strange thing to do
Our eyes were on the box as our horror grew and grew
How can happy ever after be true without a moment's peace

What can it mean?
What can it mean?
Ain't it funny that we're so far apart and there's still a flame in my heart

Once upon a time we gathered right here
A story told live and in the flesh the meaning of it not quite clear
Our eyes are turning inward as we come face to face with fear
Peaceful ever after flows down a lazy river near

What can it mean?
What can it mean?
Is it this or is it that
I asked everybody and I'm asking you right now
I asked my cat I asked my dog too
What did he say?
He said Rrrrrrrrrr rrrrrrrrrrrrrrr

> *Near the end of the song JOE enters. He seems quite intrigued by the petroglyphs and goes straight to them and begins examining them. He is carrying with him another deer hide similar to the ones that are hanging; this one contains the petroglyph for the teaching of the Frog Monster. This teaching includes the creation story of Manitoulin Island. He does not notice Jimmy and Elisha there as he is too caught up in trying to figure out the meaning of the petroglyphs.*

Ready or Not

JIMMY The greatest gift a storyteller can receive is a new legend and the permission to share it.

> *JOE does not notice that they are referring to him.*

(louder and directly at JOE) The greatest gift a storyteller can receive is a new legend and the permission to share it.

> *JOE looks at the deer hide he is carrying and comes to a realization.*

JOE Oh man, you mean me? I'm supposed to tell the story now? But I'm not ready. I know I said I would be ready by now… and well… you're all here 'cause you thought I would be ready by now. And honestly I'm supposed to be ready by now. But you know I'm just not—not—well ready. To tell you the truth I'm still trying to figure these out…

> *Motioning towards the petroglyphs.*

Anybody here know about the foundation teachings? 'Cause apparently they're pretty important. I mean after all they are the foundation… anybody? Okay I'll do my best to explain them but like I said, I'm not ready. Or at least not as ready as I wanted to be. As I feel like I should be.

I like to be ready. Don't you? Oh wait, are you ready? I didn't even ask. Maybe you're not ready. Maybe we should just call the whole thing off and I'll give you back your money. 'Cause like I said—but no, you're here, you're waiting. What you're saying is you're ready, aren't you? I mean really, basically. Or as ready as you're ever going to be. So there it is. We have to do it ready or not.

Foundation

Okay, just give me a minute. What did he say? What was it? Something about.... Okay... *(deep breath in preparation)* this here is the symbol for Time, this is Freedom, and this is Life. These are the Four Axes. This is Ceremony. And finally this is the Preservation of Humanity. So that's the foundation. Are we clear now? It's okay if you're not... you can tell me. I mean don't forget, I'm not even ready. Okay stay with me. We'll go through this together. Time: the foundation teachings say that time is continuous and infinite. Freedom: they say the most powerful thing any of us has is the freedom to say yes or no. So you're free to go. Or not. Or I could go and you could stay. Or I could stay and you could.... Life: what can I say? Freedom to life all the time. Simple right? Now. The four axes: the four things that must be in place to ensure total independence. Harvesting, Planting, Hunting, and Fishing—no, no, that's the wrong order and fishing is not even one of them. *(deep breath)* Okay, this is the deer shoulder so that's harvesting. Okay, spring, Planting, summer, Building, fall, Harvesting, winter, Hunting. And Ceremony. We've all been through ceremony... I think. What do you need for a ceremony? It has to be plain, simple, orderly, and sincere. And you can't go trying to find your spirituality at a ceremony; by the way, it must already be in place because a ceremony is only a celebration of spirituality. That's all.

Preserve Humanity: Go!

Is this too preachy? Because that's one thing I didn't want to do here was get all preachy about this stuff. What I wanted to do was, you know, like share what I'm learning. But not by preaching. You know how when you first learn something you can get a little... preachy? And I was listening to myself there talking about ceremony, and I thought, Joe...

JIMMY/JOE   You're sounding a little preachy here.

JOE   I bet if I were ready that wouldn't have happened, so... sorry... the thing is, this stuff isn't mystical. It's totally practical. Like... the preservation of humanity.... Practical. It's got to be done, right? The preservation of humanity. Holy crap... how can I possibly be ready for that now? I'm not even thirty years old! I can't even get a house from the Band Council! I mean, where do I start? Or have I started? How do you know if you've started? I mean does somebody say, "Okay, preserve humanity, go!" Shouldn't there be a ceremony for that or something?

Basic Needs

What did Eddie say about it? He said so many things but it was something about—it had to do with the diamond symbol, with the three parts of life: emotional and physical and spiritual—but the... physical is first. Yeah, okay. Physical first. Okay, we need clean air. Can we all just test that out? Everybody on the count of three take a deep breath, one, two, three. *(deep breath with audience)* How's everybody feel? Clean air? Clean air! Check. Now clean water.

> Looks around for fresh water but can only find an Evian bottle.

Humph. All right clean water.... Check, and good food... *(pulling out a package of wieners)* check. And finally shelter. Clean shelter. No. Good shelter. No, good clean shelter.... And shelter. *(takes a look around the space)* Okay well we kind of need to work on that one. Okay... so we're kind of ready. Clean air. Clean water. Good food. And shelter. Check.

Stumped

JIMMY   Go to the stump!

JOE   Which one? You see, traditionally our storytellers sat on stumps when they told stories. Anybody know why?

JIMMY   They were convenient!

JOE   Oh... but how do I know which stump is the right stump? What happens if you pick the wrong stump? Will that ruin the story? What makes a good stump? Humph. *(looking at the variety of stumps around the space)* Too small. Too big. Not enough bark. No bark. Too stumpy. Not stumpy enough. I'm stumped.

ELISHA   Just tell the story.

JOE   Which one? There're thousands of stories. Everybody has a story. Every thing has a story. Everybody has history, right? History. His story... his... story.... Her story. Our story. Ourstory.... Everybody has an ourstory.... Wait., how do I know which story is the right story? What happens if I pick the wrong story? Will that ruin the stump?

JIMMY   Will you forget the stump!

JOE   But you said…

JIMMY   Use a lawn chair. Use a La-Z-Boy. Get an ottoman. Just get on with it. This is only supposed to be a half-hour show!

Contradictions

JOE   Okay. You want a story? …Here's a story: I am Odawa but I do not speak my language. I am Catholic but I do not go to church. I believe in my traditions but I do not honour them. I believe in my ancestors but I do not follow them. I know of respect but do not respect it. I know of love but cannot give it. I am alive but not living my life. I am following what I cannot defeat. I believe in my path but do not know where it leads. I believe in myself but do not know who I am. I know of bravery but I am afraid. I know of humility but I am not humble. I am telling the truth of my reality to create a change.

Questions

Okay well, that's a story. But I don't think it's the one I was supposed to tell? What I wanted to do was tell a local story this summer. That's all. Simple, right? Maybe nothing is simple. Anyway I thought maybe a story about us… a creation story. So I went to Eddie and I asked him for a creation story about Manitoulin Island. And he gave me one. You see it actually starts at the base of the Menomonee Valley in what is now Ohio. But this was way back when what is now called North America was known as Turtle Island. You know, before they drew that line across there.

JIMMY   Why did they do that anyway?

JOE   I don't know. Separation. Identity. American/Canadian. Rich/poor. Tall/short. Good stump/bad stump. Audience/performer. Story-telling…. Theatre. Question: right now am I following in an oral story-telling tradition? Or am I performing in a theatrical production? Where do you draw the line between the two? And have I crossed it? What makes a storyteller?

ELISHA/JIMMY   The story!

Ohio

JOE   Ohio! Did I mention Ohio? That's where it starts. But why tell our stories anyway? I know part of it is to honour our ancestors. It's where the stories come from, right? Passed on, generation to generation. Do

I want to be the one to let them go, to forget them? I mean I'm an actor, a storyteller—at least that's what I put on my grant application for this project. That's why I'm here, ready or not, to tell a story. That's why you're here, ready or not, you were hoping for a story, or at least an entertaining evening out. And what are my descendents going to say, "What was up with him? He was a storyteller but he never told any stories! Look at this grant application! It's a lie!" Do I want to be known for the next twenty-four generations as that Lying-Grant-Writing-Non-Storytelling-Storyteller? Am I ready for that? I still have to report back to the Canada Council too. What am I going to tell them? "I wasn't ready. I'm a storyteller but I just wasn't ready to actually tell a story. It's an Aboriginal thing, you wouldn't understand." I could tell them that. That usually works.

Ancestors

Or… I could just tell you the story in honour of my ancestors. So Ohio…. How many ancestors have I got anyway? I wonder if any of them came from Ohio? Who knows? Let's see… there's my mom and dad… my grandparents and their parents and… I'm going to need a calculator.

ELISHA just happens to have a calculator.

Can somebody give me a hand?

ELISHA goes to find an audience member to help with the calculations.

Okay… are you ready? Here we go. I have two parents so press two, now they each had two parents so times that by two… 'k hold on… now there are seven teachings, four directions, and thirteen moons. What's that? Seven plus four plus thirteen is… twenty-four. Okay so we'll go back twenty-four generations just for the heck of it, so now you have to press the equal button on the calculator twenty-four more times to calculate how many ancestors I have in twenty-four generations. Now you have to get this right 'cause it affects the next part of the show…. What do you got?

Everybody waits for audience member to figure it out.

AUDIENCE MEMBER   33,554,432.

JOE   And those are only my ancestors! You've got 33,554,432 of your own. That's assuming they all only got married once! Go sit down and think about that for a while. Sure you don't want to try the stump? It helps— trust me.

Song "33,554,432 at least" Ancestorial Picnic
Written and performed by Jimmy and Elisha Sidlar

Well there's thirty-three million five hundred and fifty-four thousand four hundred and thirty-two at least. All my ancestors are coming and I'm cooking for the feast.

I got my great-great-great-great-great-great grandma's recipe for fry bread. I'm gonna make sure I make them proud, make sure that they're all fed.

Well there's another dump truck arriving in the yard with hopefully enough flour. Oh, more lard's being delivered this afternoon. Dear goodness me will you look at that hour.

I got Audrey's and Marjorie's and Rosemarie's and Bertha's and everybody's burners just a blazing. Oh you know what? We'll put the plain ones over on this side of the field and over here the ones with raisins.

It's a family reunion so gather round, grab some bread and pass it down. Songs to sing, stories to tell, some catching up to do as well.

And if anybody's looking I'll be in the kitchen cooking at the annual ancestorial picnic and if anybody's looking I'll be in the kitchen cooking at the annual ancestorial picnic

Real Time

JOE So when we're talking about ancestors and honouring our ancestors, this is what we're talking about. That's a lot of fry bread, eh?

JIMMY You're running out of time!

JOE You know there are only three real times. This is what our ancestors tell us. All thirty three million of them said it once or twice. Everything else is man-made, clocks, calendars, day timers. The only three real times are: day and night, the thirteen moons, and the four seasons. Like I said before, time is continuous. Time is infinite. You see our ancestors were smart. They knew. Right now we're in the *(insert proper moon number)* moon . The next time the *(insert proper moon number)* moon falls on the *(insert proper day)* of *(insert proper month)* will be thirteen years from now.

JIMMY We'd like to get home before that! Tell us the story!

The Story

> ***At the request of Cultural Advisor Eddie King this story has been altered from its original form in order to maintain the integrity of the oral tradition from which it came. The legend has been summarized below by Joe Osawabine.*

JOE   This story takes place in what is now Ohio. It begins one spring when the water never came. Because the people depend on this water they begin to get worried. So they decide that they need to send somebody up the dry riverbed to go and see what the problem is. A man volunteers to go and see; now in the story the man has no name.

He makes his way up the dry riverbed until he comes to the place in the river where the water is blocked. At this point he sees that a giant frog monster had damned the water up to keep for himself. So he goes and speaks to the giant Frog Monster and pleads with him to let the water go as his people depended on it. He said he would let it go if the nameless man gave him his unconditional love. The nameless man knew this was something he could not do. He decided the only option left was to battle the Frog Monster, and a great battle takes place.

Throughout this battle is when the seven Great Lakes are formed, the five Great Lakes as we know them today; however Lake St. Clair and Hudson Bay were also included at one time. As each of the Great Lakes was formed in this battle they each became symbolic of the seven Odawa values, Love, Honour, Respect, Truth, Trust, Compassion, and Patience.

Manitoulin Island was also created in the midst of this battle. At one point the Frog Monster threw the nameless man high into the air and the medicine pouch he had on his side ripped open and all his medicines fell to the ground and landed on Manitoulin. This is why so many medicines grow here now.

Soon the battle would come to an end. The nameless man had defeated the Frog Monster. The creator came to the nameless man and told him to go ahead and kill the Frog Monster for what he had done—blocking the water from the people—and the man said he could not do it, because to kill the Frog Monster now would be to go against everything the battle had stood for.

But the creator knew he could not go unpunished and made it so that all the Frog Monster's descendants would never be as great in size as he was and the people would never have to worry about water again and it would be his descendents that let the people know when the rain was coming. And to this day you can still here the frogs singing just before the rain falls.

***The legend in its original form is an important part of the story and should be told verbatim whenever possible. The legend can be obtained by contacting De-ba-jeh-mu-jig Theatre Group.

Segue

So that's the story. Good night. Drive safely... especially those of you travelling down Bidwell Road or Highway Six by Ten Mile Point... please watch for deer, thank you and Miigwetch.

Actually wait, while your still here... I've been working with this story now for a while and I still have a lot of questions about it. And since we've got a lot of heads in the circle... maybe we could... you know... well one thing is like... why is the man in the story nameless? Is that important? What if his name was like Eddie, or Clint, or Arnie, or Vin Diesel... or Segue? Speaking of namelessness though—get it? Segue? "Speaking of namelessness" it's a joke. Native storytellers always use humour. I'm being funny here people... you see a segue is like a bridge between two completely unrelated thoughts or ideas... or streams of consciousness if you will.... Writers use them when they want to uh... like segue between two thoughts. That might not necessarily be, you know... related.... See what I'm going for when I say segue? The Merriam-Webster Online Dictionary defines it as: making a transition without interruption from one activity, topic, scene, or part to another. Segue...

ELISHA   Forget the Segue!

Identity

JOE   Speaking of segues, could it mean a loss of identity? His namelessness that is. Or is it no identity? Maybe he's just forgetful? Or the people are forgetful and somehow lost his name as the story was passed. You know how that could happen? And how did they decide that this man should be the one to go upriver and find out what happened? Was it like, "We need water. Somebody should go." "Hey what about that, that... guy... what's his name?" "Oh, that nameless guy! Yeah him. He could go." And then the other people were like, "Yeah that guy, yeah the nameless guy. Let him go. Ahem ahh we'll just ah... wait here..." and is it me but wouldn't somebody have offered to go with the guy, even just because the poor sucker had no name? But no. No one offers... and he doesn't ask... our poor nameless man makes his journey... alone... "Bye... you! Watch for the deer! Better pull up a stump there Eddie, it's gonna be a long wait for ahh? You know... what's his name... man I'm thirsty..."

What's his name?

What does it mean to live without an identity? Did he go because he thought maybe the journey would define him, help him find out who he is? I mean think about it... he has no name... so that means he's probably never been good at anything. Screwed up his whole life. Never danced with a wolf or you know, sat with a bull or went crazy on a horse or drove a Pontiac or even a Cheap Cherokee. Nothing. The guy needed to change his luck, right? So he said: "Okay! I'll go. I gotta do something!" I can relate, you know. Really I'm up here all alone telling this story. The man was on the riverbed all alone. He didn't know what the problem was. I don't know what the problem is. I mean if you were to ask me right now—me, "Joe what's the problem here?" I'd have to say, "You know what? I don't know."

Alone

Here's a thought.... Maybe he goes alone because every person has internal struggles that they go through alone. Like me for instance, now, right now. You wouldn't have noticed this because I'm a professional actor, and I'm highly trained and everything, but tonight? Like since the beginning when I came in and I wasn't ready? This whole thing has been a real internal struggle. And I've been like totally alone. No offence because you're here and I know you're here I mean you're right there... and I can't pretend that you're not there because you're here and I'm talking to you and I can see you there so technically I'm not alone but internally, I mean, like deep down inside, I'm like totally alone... okay yeah so those were just lines I was delivering and actually, yeah, I helped to write them—and I wasn't actually alone when we were writing them—but now, it's wild 'cause it's like they were totally true... except for the spirits of my 33,554,432 ancestors from the past twenty-four generations, I am completely alone!

All My Relations

Is anybody else in the room wondering what I'm doing up here? You must be thinking, "What the heck did I pay good money to see this for? Who the heck does this guy think he is standing up there trying to be a traditional Native ancestorial contemporary storyteller? And he's probably got a laptop and downloads music. I bet he drove here this evening, for crying out loud!" And I'm not going to argue with you... you're right. I'm thinking the same thing. How does this old, old story relate to my everyday life now as a father, a son, a brother, a lover, a colleague, a member of the community? Ahem, an "esteemed" member of the community. Or does it relate at all? I feel like it does. But how? When a storyteller is given a new legend to share it doesn't mean that he owns it. Nobody owns these stories and yet everybody does. For the storyteller, the story is somehow a part of him. He feels it. He takes what he needs from it. And through sharing it, he invites everybody to do the same. This is its gift.

Connections

Getting back to our nameless guy. He lived without an identity but maybe he felt like he didn't want to die without one. And why do we live anyway? We live to die. I know a lot of people don't like to hear this but it's true. To fear death is to fear life. Death is only the beginning. Our body is only a shell for our spirit and when our physical body dies, our spirit, our Manitou, can cross over. This is why there is no way to say goodbye in our language. We will always see each other again, even in death. So we say Baa-maa-pii-kawaap-min. I will see you later. So to deny death is to deny life. So cheer up! What is this, a funeral? Or is it a performance, or is it a tradition? A performance? A traditional performance? Or is it a segue? That's it! No stay with me here! Life/death. They don't seem to be related... there's one and then the other. But what's in between? The mother of all segues! See? You following me here? Life is a segue between birth and death! Segue!

JIMMY   Will you forget the segue!

JOE   And while we're smack dab in the middle of our segue, and I mean both in the show now and generally here on the planet, living, Eddie says our mission... no our gitche Manitou directed mission, is the preservation of humanity. And this isn't just Eddie speaking by the way.

JIMMY   Who's Eddie?

JOE   Come on... you know. Eddie!

JIMMY   Oh... Eddie... ohhhhhh...

ELISHA   *(to JIMMY)* So now we know who Eddie is.... Who are you?

JIMMY   *(to ELISHA)* Who are you?

ELISHA   Who are you?

> *JOE watches them and is not impressed with their interruption. They notice JOE watching and settle down.*

Statistics

JOE   Anyway, we're back to the preservation of humanity. It's passed down to us from the rock teachings, known as the petroglyphs; we call them the talking rocks. The story of the nameless man comes from the talking rocks too…. This image is the Frog Monster from the Talking Rocks located in Peterborough, Ontario…. Our stories, our teachings, all the important things the ancestors wanted to pass on to us they put in the rock teachings, so that we would always have access to their wisdom. This Frog Monster, for example, is about three thousand years old, give or take a few thousand years. Down south, below that line that got drawn across Turtle Island, there are petroglyphs that are sixteen to eighteen thousand years old. A lot of the images there are the same as ours here. You know, people have been studying those petroglyphs for a thousand years trying to figure them out. Actually, not people, scientists have been studying them. And okay maybe not for a whole entire thousand years because first contact was only five hundred and twelve years ago and it probably took them the first hundred years to find the petroglyphs and then it was probably another fifty years or so before they got curious about them and they had to talk to their scientists and say, "So what's with all these, like, things on this rock? Could you study them for a few hundred years and see if you can figure out what they could possibly mean? And whatever you do, don't ask the people who made them!"

JIMMY   Yeah… why didn't they ask us?

JOE   I don't know… maybe they couldn't remember our name.

JIMMY   Actually, Joe, it was May, 1954. That's when they found them. A coupla guys on their lunch break.

JOE   Were they lost?

JIMMY   The guys or the glyphs?

Preservation of Humanity

JOE   What was I talking about? Oh yeah, the preservation of humanity. Kind of overwhelming when you think about it, isn't it? I mean how can I preserve humanity? I mean, like, myself alone, me. And why me? It's not like I'm nameless. I'm Joseph David George Osawabine! I got better things to do than to wander up dry riverbeds preserving humanity while everybody else sits there on their stumps and complains… but wait a minute. It's not just me… everybody contributes to the preservation of humanity. We're all in the circle. This outer circle is the sun, representing man. And this inner circle is the moon, representing woman. So the man

protects the woman. Not dominates, lords, or rules over, but protects the woman for the preservation of humanity. There's no single way or answer to preserving humanity either. It's a personal thing. And there's lots of ways to go about it. You could…. I don't know… ummm… well… and just because I'm standing up here talking and you're there listening doesn't mean that I have all the answers! Like I said before, if you were to ask me, Joe, right now, ten minutes later, "What is the answer?" I'd have to say, "You know what? I still don't know." This is just the process I am most comfortable with in searching at this point in my life….
I guess in a way, by putting wood on this fire I'm doing it. By sharing this story I'm doing it… by listening to this story you're doing it. Even before, when I was sharing my wiener earlier, I was doing it then too.

JIMMY You're preserving humanity by sharing your wiener?

JOE I could be… it's possible… one of the basic needs is food, right? The preservation of humanity. In a way we're all doing it all the time… or we could be…. Now that I think about it, it's simple really. It's in everything that we do, every day, all the time…. It's infinite. It's here. It's now. And it's simple.

ELISHA Aren't you forgetting something?

JOE No, are you?

ELISHA What did Eddie say?

JOE Well about what? He says a lot of things.

ELISHA About the preservation of humanity?

JOE I've just been talking about that. Where have you guys been?

ELISHA The preservation of humanity is vitally linked to…?

JOE I was getting to that!

ELISHA Then segue!

JOE Okay, okay. The preservation of humanity is vitally, vitally linked to the preservation of mother earth. If you don't take care of her, all the Band-Aids and Aspirins in the world can't help you. It's simple. We must take care of the earth.

Frog Monster

JOE A Frog Monster? Why couldn't it have been a cool monster? Like a crouching tiger monster or a hidden dragon monster. And the tiger monster could have roared to let the people know the rains were coming or the dragon monster could've spit fire. But no, it had to be a giant frog with a love complex. "Give me your unconditional love! I want unconditional love! I'm the big bad Frog Monster and I want..." I wonder if he's related to the big bad wolf... the big bad wolf wanted unconditional dinner...

ELISHA   What are you talking about?

JOE   I don't know. Monsters... dinner.... But I think part of it is that we all have to keep on fighting our own personal Frog Monster. The story doesn't tell us exactly how long the battle took. It just says the nameless man and the Frog Monster battled; they clawed the ground. They flung each other into the air and landed hard. Neither one let up until all seven lakes were created. Seven lakes, seven grandfathers, seven teachings.

Traditional Fool

JOE   Speaking of teachings, I still don't know if I'm performing in a theatrical production, or following an oral tradition? Or maybe I'm just making a traditional fool of myself orally? You know me, I just don't know.... And what about you? How's it going for you? Are you having a nice evening out listening to a story about how the Great Lakes were created? Or are you experiencing a legend thousands of years old, passed on from descendant to descendant through an oral tradition? Or are you just wondering? It's all valid. Freedom to life all the time. It's always up to you. It depends how you want to look at it. We all have the freedom to choose how we relate to our stories, or if we want to relate to them at all. Our legends are there.

Struggle

JOE   Every time I share this story or listen to it, I see how it directly relates to me, how I may be blocking the water up inside myself not even know-ing that I am depriving not only myself. I am also depriving all those around me who need that water. I struggle to be a good father for my son Jade, I struggle to forgive my own father for not being there, and to respect my mother who was there every day and still is. I want to be someone my brother can be proud of... and this story reflects my big long hard struggle to keep my Frog Monster in my pants.... I don't want to be all alone there if you don't mind.... This story has given me a means to exploring my first question tonight.... Am I an actor performing or am I a descendant of the great storytellers of our past? Or both? What is my responsibility to our stories? If I'm not sharing them who will? The battle between the nameless man and the Frog Monster continues, even now as I try to unblock the water and uncover the seven teachings within myself. As I struggle, as I continue to live with this legend I can see some of the connections. I know they are there. But I do not fully understand them. But maybe we don't have to understand everything.... Maybe it's enough to just keep on trying to understand, and if there were an absolute answer, if we ever came to a final conclusion about the meaning of our stories, the wonder of our stories would cease to exist. Thank you and good night .

JIMMY   Wait, wait, wait, hold on. That's close Joe, but it doesn't feel like the end to me.

JOE   It isn't. Sharing the story is only the beginning. The seeds have been planted, the medicine is on the island. Baa-maa-pii miinwaa ka-waap-min.

Song "Baamaapii miinwaa kaawaabmin"
Written and performed by Jimmy and Elisha Sidlar

Baamaapii Kaawaapmin
I'll see you later (I'll see you later)
I'll see you and you and you and you and you and you
And maybe I'll see you you you you you
I'll see you later (I'll see you later)

Over the moon (over the moon)
Under the sea (under the sea)
Where the whales unzip themselves
Where there was me and baby there was you

Baa-maa-pii-kawaapmin
Another thousand miles deep inside of me
To the starry side of you and I
Where the snowbirds leave their footprints on the snow
And you and I we kiss and laugh as were singing

Baa-maa-pii-kawaapmin
And maybe I'll see you and you and you
And you you you you
In the campfire in the sky
You'll have another face, another name in another place

Baa-maa-pii miinwaa kaawaabin
I'll see you later

The end.

The Petroglyphs

Time

Freedom

Life

The Four Axes

Ceremony

The Preservation of Humanity

Shannon Hengen is a Professor of English at Laurentian University, where she teaches the literatures of North America. Current research interests are Aboriginal theatre, Margaret Atwood's oeuvre, and the writing of South African poet/journalist Antjie Krog.

Born and raised on the Wikwemikong Unceded Reserve, **Joe Osawabine** first performed for Debaj at the age of twelve, in its landmark production of *Lupi, the Great White Wolf.* In the fourteen years since that performance, Joe's evolution as an artist has tracked Debaj's evolution as a theatre company. Joe assumed the responsibilities of Artistic Director of Debaj in 2004.